GOD AND THE TROUBLES OF LIFE

GOD AND THE TROUBLES OF LIFE

Paul Griffiths

Terra Nova Publications

Published in Great Britain by
Terra Nova Publications Ltd
PO Box 2400, Bradford on Avon, Wiltshire BA15 2YN

ISBN 1-9019-4909-5

Cover design: Gazelle Creative Productions
Cover printed by The Shires Press, Trowbridge, Wiltshire

Printed in Great Britain at
The Cromwell Press, Trowbridge, Wiltshire

This book is dedicated to Sarah, Daniel and Hannah

CONTENTS

INTRODUCTION

It has been said that when it comes to communicating to others about your life in God, many people are able to identify with your weaknesses, but far fewer with your strengths. Having been a preacher of sorts for some sixteen years, I have found in my experience that this is true. How well people listen when you tell them about a weakness, either in your own life or in the character about whom you are teaching; yet how frequently they seem to distance themselves when you proclaim the victorious Christian life. I suppose that is why I am so drawn to Jacob. If ever there was a failure who walked with God, then Jacob was that man!

I remember having been in a prayer meeting many years ago, which turned into a time of confession. Many of those present came under the conviction of the Holy Spirit, stood up, and confessed their sins to God. The turning point came when one person present said that he had a problem with pornography, and described the way in which he had succumbed to it over recent months. One man's brokenness—and honesty about his failure—sent a freeing wave through the group. A study of the life of Jacob can carry out the same liberating work for us, so that we, too, can be free to confess before God those things which hinder our relationship with Him.

Jacob was a man whose life and walk with God seemed to encounter all the 'ups and downs' of life—particularly the 'downs'. Here is a man who knows what it is to sin again and again in the same area: a man who knows what it is to suffer some of the great tragedies of life—the rape of a daughter, the death of a wife and son, and famine. His family life was difficult. He had parents who were far from perfect, and a brother who wanted to beat the living daylights out of him. He himself spoilt his children, to the point of tragedy.

The Genesis account tells us that it did not stop there. As well as having many troubles in his life, for most of his days he also had God to contend with—God, who was committed to the inclusion of Jacob in His purposes, and to the work of moulding him into the man that He wanted him to be. We see him wrestling with God, and being tested by God.

This theme, and the teaching in this book, began in my own church as a preaching series, one which I greatly enjoyed delivering, partly because I found it beneficial to look at one of the great men of God and to find that he was a failure (just like me), yet a failure who was allowed to walk with God. Such a discovery is a source of hope! Now I trust that you, too, may find both strength for one more day in your life, and a greater assurance in your pilgrimage with God, as you walk with Jacob through many of life's valleys.

Many people helped me as I wrote this book, and I express my thanks to them all: to my then vicar, for allowing me to preach from the life of Jacob; to my church, St. James in Bream, for being the guinea pigs; to my friends Steve and Viv, for doing some of the preliminary editing; and to my family, for encouraging me in this project.

On one particular day—a very difficult day in Jacob's life—he had just been forced to leave home because all his deceitful actions were catching up with him. On that day, God came to him: into the mess, into his life, and into his future. No, it did not make life from that moment into a bed of roses, but it did make it a life truly worth living. As you read about Jacob's story, let me encourage you to open your heart—so that the God who came to Jacob might come to you. God is more than able to help us during our times of trouble.

A biblical reference is provided at the head of each chapter and it is suggested that this passage should be read first.

One

PORTRAIT OF A FAMILY

Genesis 25:19–27:46

If I were to ask you to describe your home life, would you say that your home was like any of these models, some inspired by media examples?

The 'Happy Family'

A good home, where mum and dad get on with each other, where the children are all achievers and there is normally harmony and laughter. This is the home where dad could easily have been a stand up comedian. Happy faces and happy children: this is the team that works together.

The 'Strange Family'

Do you remember the *Addams Family* show? The only word to describe this is 'weird'. The parents are weird, your relatives are weird and so are the children. The only thing that is not weird about this family (but is perhaps the most weird thing of all) is that one of the family is normal: probably you.

The 'Traditional Family'

Dad goes to work and mum stays at home. This is the place of the extended family. A strong sense of community exists across the generations. 'Get togethers' are normal, and so are the sharing of life's lessons and experiences with one another. Remember the television series *The Waltons*?

The 'Troubled Family'

This is the unhappy home, a type that is becoming very familiar. It is the home where there is fighting and great disharmony. It is a home where there may be physical violence. This is the home of trouble, where the children have followed their parents' bad example and become difficult and disobedient. This can be seen in how they easily break the law and discard relationships.

The 'Betrayed Family'

This is the home that is marked by real or alleged deceit, and by others having to live with the consequences of it. It could be the deceit of an extra-marital affair, financial wrongdoing of some sort, or some other kind of law-breaking. In this home, there is the fear of being found out and, when revelations occur, feelings of betrayal arise.

The 'Incomplete Family'

In this home there has been separation, divorce or the death of either husband or wife; or one party working away, perhaps. There can be many reasons for the incompleteness, but there is someone missing.

Does any one of these models, or combination of them, begin to describe your own family—either the family you grew up in, if you are single, or the family you have helped to build?

The home is a very precious and special place. It is the place where, as children, we should find our security and nurture. It is the place where we are taught the first lessons of life, and where we are given examples of parenting and human interaction which give a considerable push to how we will act towards and treat others. It is normally the place to which we will tend to gravitate. This should be the place where we know that we will find acceptance, whatever happens; the place to which we can return when we are at our lowest or most vulnerable.

The home and family unit provides part of the vital fabric of society, which family breakdown has tended to destabilise. Such is our valuing of the family as an institution that a government can hope to win votes by giving tax concessions to married families, and benefit to those in one parent families who stay at home to look after their children. When someone is described as homeless, we consider it to be a personal tragedy for that individual.

What I want to do in this chapter, is to invite you to consider what we should expect to find in the home. What are the characteristics of a *normal* family? To help in this task, we will look at the home life of Jacob and see what it teaches us about the normal family home. What I hope we will be able to do, is become a 'fly on the wall' of next door; to manage, without their knowing, to peer through their curtains and see how they relate to one another.

To give the game away right at the beginning, I want to see where they have cobwebs and how big those cobwebs are; to detect the cupboards which house their skeletons. My aim in doing this is to help us appreciate exactly what a normal family looks like, to give us hope for our own family, to challenge us where we need to be challenged, and to comfort us where appropriate.

So let us look at a portrait of a normal family or, to put it another way, let's burst the bubble on 'they all lived happily ever after'.

A HOME WITH IMPERFECT PARENTS

There have been a number of press stories about ministers and other church leaders who have resigned for reasons of misconduct. In one such case, the church secretary, with whom the minister had allegedly been having an affair, said, "You don't have to be good to be a Christian." In one sense she was right, wasn't she? Without condoning this or any kind of sin, it is true to say that a Christian is a forgiven sinner—and when it comes to parenting, you certainly do not have to be perfect to be a parent!

In the biblical account of Jacob, we see at once that his parents were very far from being perfect parents. Consider their weaknesses. His father, Isaac, was prepared to lie about the nature of his relationship with his wife—in order to save his own skin. Conscious both that his wife was a beautiful woman, and that should the local king (Abimelech) become besotted with her, his life would be placed in jeopardy, Isaac did what his father Abraham had done with his wife Sarah, when he was in a similar situation: he lied. (See Genesis 26:7.)

He was also a man who allowed his appetite for red meat to distort his relationship with his sons. (See Genesis 25:28.) Esau was a 'man's man'; Jacob one for the kitchen. Isaac loved red meat, the kind that Esau could bring him. Such a son won favour with his father, to the detriment of the younger.

As a result of the overwhelming bias Isaac had toward Esau instead of Jacob, he sought to thwart the purposes of God, and to have Esau receive the family blessing in place of Jacob. When

Esau and Jacob were born, a prophecy had been received, which indicated that Jacob, although the younger, would become the greater of the two. He was to receive his father's special blessing—just as Isaac had received his, instead of his older brother Ishmael. Probably as a result of blatant favouritism, Isaac determined to give it to Esau instead of Jacob. (See Genesis 27:4.)

Rebekah's imperfections can be seen in the way that she, too, fell into the trap of favouritism with her boys—loving Jacob more than Esau. Whether this was because, having been present at the time of the prophecy, she knew him to be the key person in the next phase of God's work in the world, we do not know. Perhaps she was simply reacting against her husband's bias. Perhaps, as the boys grew up, she saw that Jacob had the potential to love God, and she may have warmed to that, whereas Esau seemed to want nothing to do with the things of God. We cannot be certain of the reason for her bias in favour of one of her sons, but we can observe that she, like her husband, divided the family. (See Genesis 25:28.)

Her imperfection as a wife can also be seen in her scheming against her husband, seeking to deceive him. (Genesis 27:5–17.) Rebekah overheard Isaac say that he was going to give Esau the family blessing. Her response to this was to deceive her husband by arranging for Jacob to disguise himself and take in the meal his father had requested from Esau. Why she did not talk it through with Isaac, why she simply determined to deceive him, why God allowed her success, we do not know. All we are told is that with the help of Rebekah, and at her instigation, Jacob deceived Isaac and so received the family blessing.

In the Epistle to the Colossians, the Apostle Paul gives us his code of conduct or 'house rules' for family life. To summarise, he teaches that the home is to be marked by people *giving themselves* one to another. Husbands are to give themselves to their wives, loving them as themselves. Wives are to give themselves to their husbands. Dads and mums are to devote themselves to their children. The family as God intended it to be is marked by sacrificial mutual love, and respect for each member.

Sadly for Jacob, the home environment in which he grew up was not like this. Perhaps this was part of the reason that he turned out as he did. Did he favour his own youngest son Joseph because he knew the heartache of being the smaller and less significant one? What problems that caused for Joseph! Was his scheming to get the birthright off his brother and the ultimate family blessing off his father inspired by his feelings of loss in regard to his father's love and his desire to have, therefore, what was his by divine right? His mother's encouragement to deceive was symptomatic of a deeper malaise.

Some have concluded that Jacob's attitude of deception, which had its origin in his family home, was an attitude that Jacob had to fight against for the whole of his life. His parents, too, paid a heavy price for their behaviour: two sons who sparred with each other; the elder rebelling; the forced absence of the younger one, who for his own safety was moved away to relatives—and this a great loss for Rebekah, in that she never saw her son again.

A little while ago, my grandmother told me about a family where the husband walked out on his wife and children. He and his wife had had a row and he stormed off out of the house. The man's pride prevented him from going back and receiving forgiveness. From that moment to the present day, he laments this inability for causing him the greatest of all losses. He could not say 'sorry', so he could not receive forgiveness. For marriages to survive, and for imperfect parents to parent, forgiveness has to be at the very heart of our lives—we have to be ready to acknowledge the mistakes we make, and prepared to confess them, receive forgiveness and start again.

The great failing of Isaac and Rebekah was not that they were imperfect (we all are!) but that, along the way, as they discovered their various imperfections, they never confessed them as faults, nor said sorry, nor received forgiveness from their partner or God. Such attitudes produced the environment in which Jacob grew up. **A normal family is a family with imperfect parents.** A Christian family is a family with imperfect parents, who receive and practice forgiveness and are open to being changed by God.

A HOME WITH DIFFERENT AND DIFFICULT CHILDREN

Twins was one of the great films of the 1980s, starring Danny de Vito and Arnold Schwarzenegger. The story depicts the exploits of two different and difficult lads—one who seemed to embody all the good and pleasing characteristics of his parents, and the other all that was bad and undesirable. One was an angel, the other seemed thoroughly evil. Either Isaac or Rebekah might well have described their children in such contrasting terms.

In every way, Esau and Jacob were different: physically,

17

spiritually, emotionally and concerning their attitudes. When Esau was born, he was hairy and red, hence his name Esau, meaning 'hairy'. (His nickname 'Edom' means 'red one'.) As he grew, his physique became that of the athlete, the hunter, in sharp contrast with that of Jacob.

Spiritually, they differed dramatically, as well. Jacob coveted his brother's birthright. He probably longed to see the prophecy fulfilled in his own life. As we see from his activities, once he is removed from his home he is revealed as one who naturally calls on the name of God. Esau, on the other hand, is one who cares little for spiritual things. We are not told of any occasion when he prays to God or seeks him. One was loved by God, the other hated. (See Malachi 1:2–3.)

Emotionally, they are different. Esau enjoys the company of men; Jacob that of women. Esau is one who can be controlled by his emotions, whereas Jacob can control his. Although both men experience emotional highs and lows, Esau seems to have emotions that are on the world's greatest roller-coaster. They are up and they are down, usually, in the same day. Esau wears his heart on his sleeve, but Jacob keeps his heart behind closed doors. Esau lives for the present; he is controlled by the sensuous, and is more than happy to do things he knows will upset his parents (marrying badly). Jacob is cleverer than Esau, knows where he is going, and does all within his power to get there. He is a schemer, who values highly the family tradition of a walk with God. Esau does not care about this, hence the condemnation in Hebrews 12. Unquestionably, they are a difficult pair! There is, between them, a real rivalry.

There was a battle in the womb for pre-eminence, and it seems that there was the same battle in the early years of their lives. Esau used his brawn, Jacob his brains. Unhappily for Esau, he failed to understand what was really at stake, until too late.

Such was their rivalry that, on being deprived by his brother of the family blessing, Esau exploded—to the point at which he would have been willing to kill Jacob. With Esau, further difficulty arose from his decision to marry into the wrong kind of family. (See Genesis 28:9.) Esau's taking wives from the Hittites and the Ishmaelites was a source of great grief for his parents, and we are not surprised to learn that this was really an act of revenge against them. Worldly minded, Esau rejected the family heritage and part in the purposes of God. The family tradition had been one of allegiance to the God of Israel, yet Esau decisively rebelled against this. In practice, that probably meant that, as the years went on, Esau stopped worshipping with his parents. To all intents and purposes he became a backslider.

Jacob, on the other hand, was someone who could never be trusted. He might be scheming or up to something behind your back. He might say one thing to your face but be thinking and planning something completely different.

When I was at theological college, the Principal used to say that there were two great disciplines in life. The first was that of marriage; the second, and greater, discipline was that of children. This was the case, for good and bad, in Jacob's home.

For Jacob, as the central character of this narrative, the consequence of such an upbringing was that he developed an attitude of self-reliance. *He* would do it, and do it *his* way, regardless of what God said. He had experienced rejection from his father, because he was not quite there, physically. He knew what it was to live in the shadow of a brother who, in their world, excelled well beyond himself. Although knowing himself to be the one about whom a prophecy had been given, he saw his father seek to thwart God's plans. He, like his brother, saw his parents engage in conflict and deceit and live in great disharmony.

For Jacob's parents, parenting led primarily to heartbreak. Many a night, Isaac and Rebekah would have gone to sleep with tears in their eyes. When children do the opposite of all that you have taught them, deliberately set out to hurt you, fall out with one another, and one of them gives up faith, what else is there but empty nights of pain and loneliness?

Certainly, they were to some degree responsible for what their children became—but not totally. Their children were, in some measure, responsible for their own patterns of behaviour. Perhaps you can identify with some of the dysfunctional features of that family: the disharmony, rebellion, unfaithfulness, mistrust, and the sense of disappointment in other family members.

If you recognize any of this from your own experience, please hear me when I say that God knows how you feel. He knows both what you have already endured and what you are going through at this very moment. In Psalm 34, David says that:

The Lord is close to the brokenhearted and
saves those who are crushed in spirit.

I encourage you to seek God today. Take your tears to him. Probably this will not make the situation become a bed of roses, but what it will do is cause it to become a place where you know the comfort and resources of God.

For Jacob's brother, what was it like? He was the favourite. By natural standards and cultural protocol, he was the one who would continue the family line, yet his is the story of one who, in the purposes of God, was to take second place to his younger, scheming, deceiving brother. Should we simply say that he deserved all that he got, because he acted so carelessly with his birthright? Should we say this was the purpose of God and that's that? There is mystery here, and much that we are not told. But would we be wrong to suggest that even he had a place and a part to play in the purposes of God? How difficult it is to live in a place where dreams and best hopes have been crushed. Yet anything is possible with God, who redeems people and situations, wherever there is a willingness to return to Him.

Even if your experience of family life has not been as bad as that of Isaac and Rebekah, Esau and Jacob, from what we have seen already, there are lessons here for us to learn. Difficult children are sometimes par for the course. Parenting can include sleepless nights and broken hearts. We must develop big, loving hearts and be ready to persevere with a willingness to love despite all difficulties. We must celebrate the differences between our children, not condemning any of them for their inadequacies, certainly not comparing one of our children unfavourably with another. Also, as much as is possible, we are to teach our children to rejoice in the success of their siblings, and never to despise their victories or gloat over their mistakes. Moreover, we need to understand the weaknesses of our children, seeking to the best of our ability to nurture them in those areas. Finally, we are to give them the best example we possibly can.

In *Twins*, Danny de Vito and Arnold Schwarzenegger came to a place in life where they needed each other, and where they wanted their parents. One of the goals of our parenting, and of our family life, should be to nurture long-term mutual love and care in our own families.

A HOME WHERE THINGS GO WRONG
There was a remarkable news report of a woman who, on the day that she discovered she was pregnant, learned that she had cancer

of the breast. The reason for the media attention, some ten months after the event, was the remarkable fact that the woman and baby were now both doing fine. One of the doctors who had attended the woman was interviewed, and the thing that he remarked on more than anything else was the dilemma the woman faced all those months ago. Would she wait and have chemotherapy after her child was born, and so not risk the child's life? Or would she have an abortion and then carry on with the chemotherapy? Would she have the treatment and attempt to keep the baby, hoping that it would not be damaged by the cancer or the chemotherapy? What a dilemma! What a devastating place to be!

In family life, if yours is anything like mine, you will know that difficult dilemmas—even if not as serious as this one—are part of daily living. Coping with things going wrong is all part of family life. Jacob's home life experience illustrates this undoubted truth.

We are given four examples of things going seriously awry. The first occurred before Jacob was born. For twenty years, his mother had been barren. Imagine that—twenty years of monthly cycles, a day late, a week late, could it be? No. What were they to do? Get the maidservant to bear an heir? Modern couples may have IVF or sperm tests, but there was no clinical solution for them. God sometimes answers prayer for healing of barrenness. Should they pray and trust God? What was it they were supposed to do? (Genesis 25:21.)

Then, some time after the children were born, and life had seemed to be treating them well, a famine swept across the land. (See Genesis 26:1–4.) There would have been no food for grazing, no work to be done, no food for living. Others were going to Egypt: should they go, too? They could lose all they had if they were to remain in their home country, but then they could lose it all by going away. Would they find the right place to stay? Would they be accepted by a foreign community? What were they to do?

They decided to stay, and sit it out in Canaan. That decision produced problems, as well. Initially, it seemed to have been a good idea. They prospered incredibly, but, sadly for them, their neighbours perceived this turn of events as unfair. So much were they envied that, finally, their neighbours asked them to leave. Imagine that: being asked to uproot yourself and leave what has been a very profitable place for you. Where would they go now? Would they be accepted in a new setting, with all these riches? Imagine having to cope with no longer being wanted.

Lastly, there were the dilemmas that came from having more than was needed. (See Genesis 26.) How much Isaac had inherited from his father Abraham we are not told, but, under the blessing of God, Isaac's standard of living had soared. He became one of the richest men in the area. Great power and great responsibility came with such riches, as did some new problems! How should the family act toward its neighbours? How should they treat people? Should they use their power for their own ends, or aim to operate it for justice? There is a very contemporary ring to such issues.

When Sarah and I married, the minister who spoke at our wedding commented on the way our circumstances would often change through life. Such changes would sometimes be good, but sometimes bad. There would be times when I would be devastated, times when Sarah would be overwhelmed by the events of life; times when both of us would be out of our depth, crushed by the flow of life. Through no fault of our own, in ways which were totally out of our control, we would be broken by life. The Genesis narrative makes it abundantly clear that such was the experience of Jacob's family, and it is the experience of most normal families. Often, when things go wrong, you find yourself out of your depth.

Ecclesiastes Chapter 3 teaches that there are seasons to life: some seasons that are good and others that seem bad. The timing of these seasons is out of our control. To some, this thought brings only despair and distress, for they conceive the controlling power as 'fate' or mere chance; yet, for others, this is good news, for they see, behind all times and seasons, the hand of God.

Unlike many homes today, the home in which Jacob grew up was one where the things that went wrong would have been understood in terms of the purposes of God, for such was the world-view in which he and his parents lived. When they were going through their trials, 'good news' might not have been the right term, yet the mishaps and problems they encountered would have been, for them, opportunities to understand what it was that God wanted to do with them, bring God again into their situation and re-orientate themselves to Him.

How much we need to use our times of hardship, difficulty and problems as times of opportunity, when we can ask God to come and take control, discerning His purpose in the midst of all that is happening to us.

For Jacob, the family tradition of faith in God would have given him a path to follow when life became extremely difficult. As we will see later, this is exactly what he did after being forced to flee his home, following the family blessing deception.

This way of faith in God and His good purposes for us, in good times and bad alike, should be our way of life and the example we give to other members of our family. The 'normal' family is the family where things go wrong. The Christian family is one where God is invited and His purpose sought. In both hard times and easier times, we need to go to God in prayer, to understand the Scriptures, and seek the counsel of other believers.

A HOME WITH PROMISE

My wife and I attended the wedding of one of her relatives. To say the least, it was an unusual wedding. The joyful tone was set as soon as the the bride did a banner waving dance during the worship time at the start of the service. The bride's uncle, who conducted the service, inadvertently omitted something (though as he had come from abroad, we understood this.) So, at the signing of the register, the registrar had to mention to them that they were in fact not yet married, and still had to say one or two other things. To cap it all, when friends of the bride and groom said a blessing over them, one member of the party stood so close to the candles that a little fire began and had to be stamped out!

Yet the most unusual thing was the intensity of the service, and the amount of time in it that was directed to God. At some points it would have been hard to gauge whether this was a service of worship or a wedding. Worship was central. After the vows had been made in the presence of God, friends from the church were invited to pray for the bride and groom. An open invitation was given to the congregation for prayers to be offered. One or two people gave prophecies. The minister brought what he believed was a word from God for the couple.

The key thing was the fact that such prominence was given to God, with honest and open hearts—not just for show, or as a formality. The little mistake and mishap on the day might have seemed unpromising, but they did not matter.

I believe that that couple has *promise*, and a *special* promise from God. Why? Because they sought at the very beginning of their marriage to give God His rightful place.

To have ascribed to God His rightful place of authority would have been the practice of Jacob's family. They were heirs of God's promise to Abraham, members of God's chosen people. Hence, it was a family with a very special promise. They were imperfect parents and they had difficult children; they went through times when things went unexpectedly wrong—but, in the midst of it all, they acknowledged God in their lives.

We see them as a family of promise during that great test of barrenness, lasting some twenty years, when they called on God. Scripture tells us that Isaac prayed. Twenty years of praying to God on a single issue: that is a sign of promise in a family. (See Genesis 25:21.)

During the time of pregnancy discomfort, they called on God. Remember the great fighting that was going on in Rebekah's womb? Her response to it all was to listen to what the Lord had to say about it. (Genesis 25:22.)

Although Rebekah's deception of her husband is not commended, the reason for it was probably that she believed, and wanted to see fulfilled, the prophecy of God for her family.

When prompted by God in a dream, after his escape from his brothers' clutches, Jacob responds to God with an open heart.

But Jacob's family was a family of promise not only because they called on God, but because *God had called on them.* During the famine, God had said to them that they were to stay in Canaan, an instruction that led to great blessing. (See Genesis 26:1–4.) The reason they prospered as they did was not the farming and business skills of Isaac, but rather that God had put His hand on them to bless them. (Genesis 26:12.) The prophecy given to Jacob came because God had chosen that family, following on from His election of Abraham, and then Isaac, to be the means through which He would express His covenant, calling a people for Himself and, ultimately, a people from whom Jesus would come.

Jacob's family were blessed with promise, both because they called on God and because God had called on them.

GOD IN THE HOME

So what a great environment this really was for Jacob to be brought up in: a home with God at its heart. Despite all the problems, trials and tribulations, and the relational difficulties we observed, this was a home with purpose, meaning and a role to fulfil in this world. Despite all their many imperfections, they responded to God. This can be our source of hope and promise, as well.

Through the death of Jesus Christ, God has called on us—both individually, and collectively, as family units. We can all be 'families of promise' as we respond to the initiative of God, inviting Him into our lives.

You might feel that, although able to identify with the first three characteristics of this family, you are not able to say with honesty that you are a family of promise. The invitation of scripture to all of us is:

Be still, and know that I am God [Psalm 46:10].

Let the peace of Christ rule in your hearts... [Colossians 3:15].

Do not be anxious about anything, but in everything, by prayer and petition, with thanksgiving, present your requests to God.
And the peace of God, which transcends all understanding, will guard your hearts and your minds in Christ Jesus
[Philippians 4:6–7].

For he chose us in him before the creation of the world to be holy and blameless in his sight... [Ephesians 1:4].

For we are God's workmanship, created in Christ Jesus to do good works, which God prepared in advance for us to do [Ephesians 2:10].

Let me encourage you to become a family of promise by inviting God into your home now.

Over the ten years Sarah and I have been married, we have lived in six homes. As you can imagine, that has meant an awful lot of packing and unpacking. One of the advantages of moving as often as we have (probably the only one) has been that we are continually having to assess the things we own. Is it time to get rid of them now? Shall we keep them a little longer? Should they now take pride of place? Having an attic full of things, fit to burst, has never been one of our problems. In other attics I have seen, you wonder how much rubbish needs to be sorted and cleared out.

A 'normal' family is marked by many imperfections, as was the family of Jacob, but like his family, can still enjoy the promises and blessings of God.

So I conclude this chapter by encouraging you to engage in an emotional, spiritual and physical 'attic assessment and clear out'. What I mean by this is that, from time to time, we need to reflect on the life of our family and see what there is there that is good, and what is bad; to see if there are treasures to be given pride of place or rubbish which needs to be discarded. We are to honour principles that are good, and of God, and to confess and get rid of our bad and damaging habits.

PRAYER

Heavenly Father, we invite you into our family.
Come and be involved in everything that goes on here.
We pray that we may know your forgiveness and wisdom.
As parents, we thank you for our children, and pray that
they might follow your ways, and become all that you
created them to be. In difficulties, help us to be aware that
you are near, and that you love us with perfect, infinite love.
Make us a family of promise.

Two

ONE BIG, BAD HABIT

Genesis 27:1–28:6

Christians are people who still sin! If we are honest with ourselves, we have to admit that we all know what it means to face temptation and, sometimes, lose. Such falling into sin is what is happening in the passage we consider in this chapter. Jacob, the man of God who walked with God for over one hundred years, is committing a sin. What I want to do in the following pages is to consider the anatomy of sin, identify the particular sin into which Jacob fell, suggest why he was beaten by it, and look at the consequences of such a failure. Before we look at the passage, though, I want to make a few introductory comments about it, and about the issue of sin.

First, we need to remember that sinning really is a problem for *everyone*. Never sinning does not mean that one is spiritual, but rather that one is dead! We read in 1 John 1:8 that, *If we claim to be without sin, we deceive ourselves and the truth is not in us.* Second, when it comes to sinning, the areas for potential defeat are numerous. Although we will be focusing in on one particular sin here, the New Testament gives us a list of over a hundred ways in which one can fall. So do not feel left out—Jacob's sin might not be your sin, but the same principles still apply. Third, when it

27

comes to the *practice* of sinning, it is possible to sin at any time and in any place. From the passage, you will note that Jacob sinned whilst in the family home; it is also possible to sin at work, in school, after going to Spring Harvest, or when coming home from church. There is no place, and no time, when one is safe from temptation and sin. Fourth, as we come to look at the ugly side of our walk with God, it is important that you remember that God loves you *even though you sin*. Jesus died for you, with God knowing that even after you had come to love and know Him you would still walk, at times, in the dark. God is not going to give up on you. Philippians 1:6 promises that God, who has begun a good work in you, will carry it on to completion. From the passage, you will see that, although Jacob sinned, God still blessed him, used him and loved him. Fifth, if you are a student of theology, you will be aware that we are considering the biblical doctrine of 'sanctification'— the outworking that occurs between being redeemed and finally glorified.

So let us look at Jacob's sin. What happened when he entered the battle zone and lost?

NAMING THE SIN

A little while ago, I heard that a Christian book warehouse near my home was closing down. As a result, they were selling many books at a ninety per cent discount. Because of my ministry, and love of theological books, I found that an irresistible offer. I had been told by the proprietors to make sure I took advantage of it. At church, a couple of weeks later, I was told that the sale had already begun. So, at nine o'clock on the Monday morning, I phoned the warehouse to check that this was true, and to arrange a time when I could come and look around. It would be an understatement to say that I felt put out when I was told by the person who answered the phone that, although they were having a sale, she was sorry, but I would not be welcome at the warehouse. It was closed to the general public. Yes, but I was an account holder. She was sorry; I would have to take it up with their bookshops, which were being offered all their reduced stock.

For the next hour or so, I telephoned various people to find out the full picture. What I learned was that others had been in the warehouse, enjoying the 90% discount, during the previous week. What I also discovered was that one of their shops, where I had previously bought books, had no intention of passing on any of the discount to others. I was feeling angry at all this inconsistency, to say the least. But what could I do? The woman had said that they were not welcoming people to the warehouse this week. What if I went to the warehouse? I had not given her my name; I could say that I had been given an invitation several months ago, and then see what I could get. No one would know that I had phoned earlier. She had said that they had had lots of calls. It might not have been completely honest, but it did not seem totally dishonest either.

The temptation to deceive was what Jacob faced and succumbed to, on what had begun as a very normal family day. (See Genesis 27:1–40.) Jacob's mother, Rebekah, had overheard Isaac promise to give the special family blessing to Jacob's brother, once Esau had served Isaac one of those red meat meals he liked so much. Verses 5–12 tell us that, when she told Jacob, he agreed with her that the only way to deal with the situation was to ensure that he got the blessing before Esau. After all, God had promised it to Jacob at birth. Rebekah and Jacob knew that such trickery would not be easy, but with sheep hair for body hair, Esau's clothes to give him his smell, and Isaac's eyesight so poor, they could do it. They did.

The dictionary definition of 'deceive' is to mislead purposely. That is what Jacob did, on that seemingly normal, but highly significant, day. He deceived his father, in misleading him as to his true identity, and he deceived his brother, taking from him that which was his. As Esau said (in Genesis 27:36), he did that which was true to his name: *"Isn't he rightly named Jacob? He has deceived me...."*

Through this act of deceit, Jacob joined a particular group of biblical characters: people who, for various reasons, tricked others. Abraham, we have noted, deceived kings as to the nature of his relationship with his wife, claiming her to be his sister so that his life might be spared. Ananias and Sapphira, two early church landowners, tried to deceive the church community by making them think that they were more generous than they were. Tobiah and Sanballat, two government officials, continually attempted to trick Nehemiah into stopping the great work that he had begun. The serpent sought to deceive Adam and Eve in regard to that which God had actually said, so that he might rob them of the precious gift of His presence. It seems that there are many ways that one can deceive others, and many reasons for doing so.

In identifying Jacob's sin as such, the question we must ask ourselves is this: are we deceivers? As we look through our lives, now and in the past, are we aware of times and occasions when we have deceived people? Have we intentionally tried to pull the wool over their eyes? Are we wearing any masks that portray us other than as we actually are? When we come before God, do we pretend to be what we are not? At church, do we use spiritual language or worship actions to mask a heart that is dead and cold? Are there actions that need to be confessed to our partners? With people at work, have we declared ourselves to be Christians? In regard to our speech, is what we say truthful? The Bible says that God 'abhors lying lips'. Are ours? Do we exaggerate the facts? Do we tell lies? Do we break confidences—whether for our own ends, to stir trouble, or through carelessness in our speech?

As I have already noted, Jacob deceived both his father and brother. He was one who abused the truth for his own ends. The challenge of the passage is to focus us on such activity in our own lives.

A LIFELONG BATTLE

One of the most significant moments in the life of Jesus, and of the disciples, occurred at Caesarea Philippi. It was there that Peter made the inspired, supernatural confession, "You are the Christ, the Son of the living God", in response to Jesus' question as to who people were saying he was. (See Matt. 16:13ff.) In the verses which follow, Peter says of Jesus' suffering and death, "Never, Lord! ...This shall never happen to you." Jesus' response, on the surface, appears to be an 'over the top' reaction. In full view of everyone, he rebuked Peter, saying, "Get behind me, Satan!" How are we to understand this response of Jesus? Was it 'over the top'? Not at all, for what Jesus saw was something that had been going on all his life: a satanic attempt to tempt him away from fulfilling his messianic mission in God's way. That was what he had faced during the temptations in the wilderness. It had happened at the feeding of the five thousand. It would happen at Gethsemane. It was happening now. It seems that Jesus faced the same challenge throughout his life.

From Jacob's story, we can see that he had a lifelong battle with one particular sin, which he (unlike Jesus) lost on many occasions. Hence my title for this chapter, 'one big bad habit'. For it seems that deceit was, for Jacob, a *habitual* sin. We begin to discern this from Esau's words on how being tricked out of the special family blessing was not the first time that he had been deceived by his brother. Jacob had also deceived him of his birthright. As the older brother, Esau had special rights. Jacob wanted those rights, and believed the prophecy gave them to him. Not waiting for God to sort it all out, he tricked Esau out of them for a bowl of soup. (See Genesis 27:36 and 25:29–34.)

"He has deceived me these two times: he took my birthright, and now he's taken my blessing!"

We see Jacob again falling into the act of deception several years later, whilst residing with his uncle, Laban. Following Jacob's forced departure from his father's house, Jacob heads for his uncle's home, there to fall in love and marry Laban's daughter. It is not long, however, before Jacob is up to his old tricks again. We learn that Jacob, having been told by God in a dream that it was time to go home, sought to build for himself a large flock of sheep, through deceptive means. (See Genesis 30:15–43.)

Whenever the stronger females were in heat, Jacob would place the branches in the troughs in front of the animals so they would mate near the branches, but if the animals were weak, he would not place them there. So the weak animals went to Laban and the strong ones to Jacob. [v. 41ff]

In 31:20, it is suggested that we further see Jacob deceive Laban, by the way that he sneaks away from the farm, not telling Laban that he is going, not giving him a chance to say goodbye to his daughters or family. [See Chapter 5 for an alternative view.]

Moreover, Jacob deceived Laban the Aramean by not telling him he was running away.

Another obvious illustration of Jacob the deceiver at work is his attempt to fool and soften his brother, when he comes to meet with him in his great act of reconciliation (Genesis 32–33.) Not wanting to be seen as wealthy, and wanting to woo Esau, Jacob cannily plays his cards close to his chest as he encounters his long-time angry brother. [Again, see Chapter 5 for alternative view.]

That night Jacob got up and took his two wives, his two maidservants and his eleven sons and crossed the ford of the Jabbok. After he had sent them across the stream, he sent over all his possessions [32:22–23].

Our sinful acts can be grouped in three categories. There are the *occasional* sins that we commit. We might lie; we might gossip; we might steal. Then there are sins that are *seasonal*. These are ones that we focus on for a considerable time, and then move on. If we are listening to God, wanting to grow in obedience, the Holy Spirit highlights the area of sin for us, so that we can repent of that sin and be forgiven. Later, He shows us other areas which we need to deal with. Finally, there are sins that we find ourselves having to focus on again and again, throughout our lives: the *persistent* sin. This is the type of sin that we see Jacob committing.

What does this mean for us? Two questions will help. Firstly, can you identify in your own life a particular temptation that you are continually falling into? It would be good to reflect on your life and see if the Holy Spirit identifies particular mistakes you commit repeatedly. If nothing else, such an exercise will help us guard ourselves for future occasions. Secondly, do name that repetitive—seasonal, or persistent—temptation. Satan unsuccessfully sought to tempt Jesus to misinterpret his task. For Jacob it was how he would see God's will worked out in his life. For Samson the issue seems to have been sexual temptation. For others it is laziness; for others, anger; and, for others, gossip. What is it for you?

Jacob fell, again and again, to the sin of deception. Such a continual falling had a devastating effect on his life. The warning of the passage is that the same could be the case for us. The challenge is to ensure that it does not.

CREATIVE MILIEU
In televised football matches, both during half time, and at the end of the game, the experts comment on what is going on. If such an analysis could take place, to explain why Jacob played as badly as he did, what would the expert opinion be?

Why exactly had Jacob acted so badly, as he deceived his father? Can we identify any particular area of weakness, or was it an accumulation of things? Is the blame to rest with the parents for the deception which took place on that day ? As we observed in the last chapter, Jacob grew up in a dysfunctional home. He had a father and mother who nurtured favourites, a father who was so sensually driven in regard to his food that he rejected Jacob in favour of his older son. Or, alternatively, are we to understand Jacob's sin in terms of an appreciation of the situation? These were desperate times: they demanded desperate measures. Under normal circumstances, Rebekah would never have considered deceiving her husband, let alone encouraging her son into sin. But he was about to give the blessing to Esau. Or is the blame to rest with an unseen character who was involved that day—Satan? After all, it was he, and he alone who is the motivating force behind so much evil. With spiritual discernment and biblical insight, we can see his activities behind the scenes.

I believe that we should not underestimate the effect that all this had on the way the game was played on the day. But I also believe that the root of the problem, the core reason why on that day Jacob did that which he did, was not because his parents had been dysfunctional, nor because the circumstances were so dire that they demanded such wrong actions, nor even because Satan was active, seeking to thwart the very purposes of God. The reason why Jacob did what he did was *because Jacob chose to follow the desires of his own sinful nature.* God had given him a prophecy, at birth, which said that he would be the greater of the two brothers. Although he was the younger one, he would be served by the older. The reason why Jacob behaved as he did on that day was that he doubted that word, and then, in his doubt, he sought to fulfil it himself.

To put it into New Testament terms, the spiritual nature was beaten by the sinful nature. As Galatians 5 says:

For the sinful nature desires what is contrary to the Spirit, and the Spirit what is contrary to the sinful nature. They are in conflict with each other, so that you do not do what you want.... The acts of the sinful nature are obvious: sexual immorality, impurity and debauchery; idolatry and witchcraft; hatred, discord, jealousy, fits of rage, selfish ambition, dissensions, factions and envy; drunkenness, orgies and the like [vv. 17,19].

Let us set this out in the order suggested by James 1:14–15. Jacob sinned when he was *motivated* by his own evil desire; he was dragged away and *enticed*; this desire then *conceived a sin* involving an act of the will, which was then followed by a *sinful action*. Hence, on the day when Jacob stands before God, it will be he—and not his parents, nor his situation, nor the evil one, who will be judged for his actions.

Several years ago, Sarah and I came across a church that was very much into inner healing. Now over the years we have actually met a lot of people who are or who have been associated with this ministry. But the particular people I have in mind here were extreme in their views—in two senses. First, they would not have held such a balanced biblical view on the cause of Jacob's sin. They would have wanted to offer a person in Jacob's position a counselling session, to help him identify the deep issues in his parents' past, or in his grandparents' past, or when he was in the womb; or they would have offered deliverance from the demon within, instead of helping the 'client' to appreciate that he was primarily responsible for his own actions. Second, they undervalued the power of the blood of Jesus Christ, and the relevance of the Cross to the believer—though they would vigorously deny this was so. For them, counselling had taken the place of the Cross and the blood, and in particular the lost sinner kneeling, ashamed and guilty, before it.

The story of Jacob is the story of a man who wilfully deceived his father and brother. It is the story of a man who needed to come to repentance, and to a point of receiving forgiveness from God. This is easier to obtain when one understands and accepts the truth of the issue. He sinned precisely because *he decided to go with the impulse of the sinful nature*.

THE FRUITFULNESS OF SIN
During the last decade of the twentieth century, one of the great public debates in Britain concerned what was termed 'sleaze'. A great outcry was raised about issues of public morality, centring on the financial and other activities of some members of parliament. This became a key General Election issue. In an effort to save face and gain political credibility, the major political parties finally called for an end to the sleaze.

When it comes to considering the price Jacob paid for his deceitful acts, what was at stake for him was something far more devastating than the media attacks which modern public figures encounter, painful as they can undoubtedly be for all concerned. Because of Jacob's deceitful actions, he was never to see his mother again. Attempting to save his life, she sent him away, and she died before he returned. There also resulted enmity between him and his brother. Esau said that he would kill Jacob as soon as he could get his hands on him. Moreover, his brother was provoked into bitterness and backsliding. Made unhappy by what he had encountered in Jacob, and by the subsequent response of the family, Esau did something which hurt his family—marrying outside his own nation. On top of all this, Jacob suffered the rejection and isolation which came from having to leave his family and live away from them for twenty years.

If we were to extend this particular study to include the whole of Jacob's life, we would see that, as a result of his other deceitful activities, Laban's sons fell out with him. Laban himself fell out with him. He saw his wife develop this habit of deceiving. (Note her denial of knowing the whereabouts of Laban's 'gods', the idols that she had stolen.) Jacob also saw his sons deceive others. What a catalogue of sad consequences!

In his letter to the Galatians, Paul says that God cannot be mocked; that a man reaps what he sows. Genesis 27 shows us that Jacob sowed to the sinful nature and reaped from that same nature. Jesus spoke of a man who, having once found buried treasure in a field, sold all that he had, that he might buy the field and so own the treasure. What the account before us shows us is that the 'treasure' Jacob sought also cost him everything that he had. Unhappily, that also included his family and kin, his self-respect, and his home. We are also shown that he even lost the 'treasure' itself, for twenty years.

In the parable of the prodigal son, Jesus spoke of all going well for the boy when he had come to his senses. The reason that he left home and spent all his money was that he was not in his right mind: he had lost all sense of reality. But when he came to his senses, he gained the opportunity to see things come right again.

In the presence of the Lord, right now, I invite you to name, in your own heart, any of your own actions that you know to be wrong, by their true names. They are sin, and as sin they will cause you to pay a heavy price—unless you take such a step. Visualise Jacob's lonely life; his heartbreak, and the sadness of his mother's face. Such desperate unhappiness is part of the price of our sin. Do not let us try to fool ourselves, but, rather, see things as they really are. It is necessary to call a spade a spade, so that we, like Jacob and the prodigal son, don't end up in pig swill.

PATH TO VICTORY

Those of you who are familiar with the speeches of the great American civil rights leader Martin Luther King, will know that one of his most memorable and inspiring addresses climaxed with his recital of the Negro spiritual:

"Free at last. Free at last. Thank God Almighty, I'm free at last."

It was a quotation which expressed the delight of the Hebrews as they came out of bondage from Egypt, and a prophetic hope King had for the civil rights movement's success in getting racial equality. Concerning Jacob, we have to be honest and say that we cannot be sure whether Jacob was ever able to make such a claim. Was Jacob free at last? Depending upon who you read, your view could be that Jacob never got there—that he died still with the same struggle as he was born with. On the other hand, some reckon that it took God about a hundred years to get Jacob into freedom. Others take a more balanced position, suggesting that although Jacob never got there, there were probably unrecorded incidents in his life when he overcame the temptation to deceive.

Should you hold either of the latter two views, as I do, the question one should then ask is, 'How did it happen?' I would suggest that at one point Jacob overcame temptation, in that he became free of his mother's influence. As Joseph removed himself from the temptation offered him by Potiphar's wife, so Jacob was removed from the inducement of his mother. True, Joseph ran, whereas Jacob was pushed, but the outcome was still the same. They got out of the fire. It is with practical intelligence that Paul warns the Corinthians not to have anything to do with those who play fast and loose with the faith.

It is also the case that a move towards victory came about *because Jacob found himself being broken by God.* In the sovereignty of God, Jacob found himself with the chief deceiver of them all—Laban. Jacob's mother grew up in the same household as Laban, so she probably learned the art of deceit from him. During the twenty years Jacob lived at Laban's house, he was deceived repeatedly. He was deceived on his wedding night, when Laban switched Rachel, whom Jacob loved, for her older and less desirable sister, Leah. Through the years that Jacob worked for him, Laban cheated him, again and again, in the matter of his wages.

These are just the events of which we are made aware.

As we think of Jacob's desperate struggle, we reflect upon our own desire to escape evil and move into the area of holiness. We may sing these well-known words: *Refiner's fire, my heart's one desire is to be holy... I choose to be holy...*, or, *Create in me a clean heart, O God.* But as we sing or pray them, the only things we are inviting into our lives are tears and difficulties—*unless* we are really open to all that God wants to do in our lives. If we are honest, do we really want the pain of brokenness before God?

Most probably, Jacob found victory in his deep and overwhelming encounters with God, for it is only in our encountering and receiving from God that true victory over temptations, sin and all evil can really begin. God's meetings with Jacob started lightly at Bethel, with his being given visions and promises—and they advanced to the point where he wrestled with God; then he never again walked in the same way as before.

What is the application of all this for us? It is that *victory is possible*. How? Through treading a similar path to Jacob—not, of course, in respect of his deceit, but as one who came to God, and who had a life-changing meeting with God. We need to be disentangling ourselves from all those difficulties which past sin may have caused, acknowledging our part in it all before God, and turning to Him for forgiveness and new life. We need to be responding to God and allowing Him to break us. We need to be seeking a deeper encounter with God, and greater awareness of His presence.

OUR VICTORY

We have looked at Jacob's one big, bad habit. In doing so, we have identified the sin he committed was that of deceit; that such a sin was a lifelong battle for him; that the cause of such sin was primarily his decision to yield to the sinful nature; we have seen the influence of his upbringing, the circumstances he found himself in, and the nature of the evil one; observed that such actions on Jacob's part cost him dearly, and that there were for Jacob occasional victories, which arose from practical and spiritual steps being taken.

In the light of all that, I want to finish this chapter by giving you three exhortations. Firstly, please allow me to remind you that, although you belong to the church of the redeemed and of the soon to be glorified, you are also a member of the church of those who are presently being sanctified.

Therefore, do all that you can to ensure that your church does not create an atmosphere where people are afraid to share or deal with their failures. Secondly, do remember that God loves you, that Christ died for you, and that the blood of Jesus is able to cleanse you from all your sin—even those sins that you commit again, and again, and again.

Finally, take some time regularly to invite God into that area of your life where any habitual sin of yours resides. He has the power and the will to deal with it, if you allow Him to do so. Talk to Him about it, and be open with Him.

PRAYER

Heavenly Father, help me to know your forgiveness;
to be filled with your Holy Spirit,
and to seek purity of heart.
Thank you that you love me,
and that one day I will be like your Son.
As I walk in that direction, be ever at my side.

Three

GOD IN MY LIFE

Genesis 28:10–22

If, next Sunday, the minister of your church were to invite you to stand up and tell everyone there about your walk with God, what would you have to say?

Would yours be the testimony of the great sprinter? Would you be able to tell the congregation, in graphic detail, about how your spiritual journey began; how, perhaps at a time of need or crisis in your life, you met with God—maybe through coming to church, or through talking with a friend? Could you describe to the fellow members of your church how you received Jesus as Lord?

Would yours be the testimony of the 'middle distance runner'? —It was not until you were in your late thirties that things started to hot up for you; following a very uneventful spiritual beginning, which in many senses determined the speed of the early years, God met with you.

Or would yours be the testimony of the 'fast finisher'? —For much of your life, Christianity has been a side issue. As you pursued your career and the welfare of your family, there has not been enough time to give adequate attention to spiritual things. You wish you could have given it more time, but special church services and semi-regular attendance were all your hectic life could give. Though that has all changed now; through early retirement, or a sudden awareness of the frailty of life and the shadowing of eternity, you have found a commitment to give your all to God. You might not have started well, you might have limped through the middle years, but now is the time for running.

Or, again, would yours be the testimony of the 'all rounder'? You found Christ in your teens, and from that day to this have given yourself to the Christian cause. No, you have not lived a perfect life, but you discovered early on that all that you needed— and all that was worth having—was found in God, so you orientated your life around Him.

What is it that you would have to say? Does any one of these profiles come close to fitting your experience? Unquestionably, they would all be represented in many congregations.

As we continue to look at the lessons we can draw from the life of Jacob, we come now to the moment when he first stood up and excitedly gave his testimony. The occasion is his coming to the house of his uncle, Laban, and being invited to stay there. Jacob's 'testimony time' is recorded in Genesis 29:13:

As soon as Laban heard the news about Jacob, his sister's son, [that he was there], *he hurried to meet him. He embraced him and kissed him and brought him to his home, and there Jacob told him all these things.*

If you are wondering about the reason for Jacob's evident lack of restraint in sharing his faith story with his uncle, and indeed that he has a faith story to tell at all, we may reasonably conclude that it arose from the encounter with God that he had so very recently experienced at Bethel. Although we do not know the actual content of his testimony, my guess is that we would not be far wrong to suggest that it was a summary of the meeting already mentioned, recorded in Genesis 28:10–22.

In this chapter we will look at what would have featured in Jacob's testimony: the consequences of meeting with God. My purpose is to encourage you, as you realise that this is the God in *your* life; so that you might have a Spirit inspired triggering of those times in your life when God has walked with you, and be challenged to seek a Jacob-type encounter with God for yourself.

As Christians, our testimonies proclaim irrefutable evidence of the truth about Christ. They declare, even to the most difficult agnostic, that there is a God. They are also a deep well of inspiration, for ourselves and for others. The psalmist often encourages the heart of one who is sad to think through the truth about God in one's life.

So what did Jacob have to say to his uncle, that, in the words of a well-known bishop, he would have been 'happy to shout across the street', on any day?

CHOSEN BY GOD

A little while ago, Britain held a General Election, the occasion when we vote for the candidate whom we think best expresses our views and belongs to the party we want to support. For those who are gripped by General Elections, one of the many highlights is staying up into the early hours of the Friday morning and listening to the results being read. Whenever there is a result to be announced, the cameras are in that particular constituency. I enjoy the focusing in on the faces of the candidates as the results are read. They tell you whether they think they have done well or badly, and if they have got the votes they had been hoping for. The winner, as we all know, is usually the person with the biggest grin—which sometimes stretches from ear to ear as the result is announced and it is formally declared that he (or she) has been elected to Parliament.

The grin of the winner, the chosen one, could well have been the look on Jacob's face as he told Laban his story. Whether Jacob was looking for God's approval on that first night away from home, we cannot be sure. Genesis 28 does not suggest that Jacob had been particularly assiduous in praying and inviting God to be involved in his life—until he makes the vow recorded in verse 20. Yet later on, recounting this incident to his family, Jacob evidently understands his encounter with God as an answer. An answer to what? He says:

"Then come, let us go up to Bethel, where I will build an altar to God, who answered me in the day of my distress and who has been with me wherever I have gone." [Genesis 35:3]

When God met with Jacob that night in his dream, the overwhelming feature of it was that he had been **elected** by God. He had somehow been *chosen*. But chosen in what sense? First of all, God had chosen him. Since his birth, Jacob had known that

41

he was special. As a child he would have been told by his mother of the prophecy given to her at the time of his birth—how God had said that he was to be head of the family. As we saw in the last chapter, Jacob's response to that prophecy was to take it upon himself to fulfil it diligently; there had been nothing that Jacob would not do to ensure that he got his inheritance. He had acted as if it all depended on him. The revelation of Bethel had been that he did not need to exercise such positive thinking and actions, for God had *already* picked him. He had been chosen by God; God had made a sovereign choice between him and his brother Esau. This was a choice that was irrevocable: a choice independent of any of Jacob's or Esau's qualities. Do you remember at school, when they played games and how you all had to stand against a wall, then get picked, one by one, for a team? Remember the feelings that came with being picked among the last? Remember the hope of being picked before the last. Jacob's experience was that he was picked first by God. He was God's special choice. It was not about self effort. Nor was it about earning God's attention and favour. It was not about being likeable, nor about putting in enough effort; it was about God and about His deciding that it was so.

Secondly, Jacob was chosen by God *for a specific purpose*. In Isaiah, the writer tells us that God's thoughts are not our thoughts and His ways are not our ways—reminding us that feeble men, with their finite minds, cannot really comprehend the plans and works of the infinite, holy creator God. This is what we become aware of as we seek to discern God's will.

The experience of Jacob exemplifies this spiritual truth. No doubt he had meditated on the prophecy many times since his youth, but from Jacob's subsequent actions we can see that he had understood it in very narrow terms. He would receive Esau's birthright, and the special family blessing. From what God said to him as he gazed at the ladder from heaven, Jacob became aware that God had intended a much more far-reaching significance than had been apparent before. This was not just about the family's sheep, slaves, tents and money. This was about the land of Canaan, which had first been promised to Abraham, then to Isaac—and was now being promised to him.

Later generations would come to see a greater significance still: this all proved to be about the kingly, Davidic line—for from Jacob would come kings and nations. Without stretching the point, we can observe that this was also about God's plan for the eventual coming of the Messiah, who would come and would bless all nations.

Little did Jacob realize that God was putting into effect the greatest of all His mighty works. This was something greater than ancient peoples could comprehend or imagine: greater than the building of the pyramids; greater than the travelling of the trade routes: God was going to do an eternal, global work, and Jacob had been chosen as His instrument in it.

Have you ever read the account of the appointment of the twelve disciples to be apostles, and wondered how they must have felt? (See Mark 3:13–14.) They had already grasped that Jesus was special, and perhaps had begun to understand the nature of his mission—the establishment and advance of the Kingdom of God. They had seen that many others wanted to be near him; they were aware of the thousands who listened to his words. Then, one day, he called some of his followers together on a mountainside, and chose for himself twelve of the disciples, to be with him and taught by him. These were the ones he now designated 'apostles'. We can well imagine the sense of specialness which would have been felt by the chosen twelve. Each might have been aware of his unworthiness, yet, at the same time, conscious of the tremendous privilege of being one of those who were now to be so very close to the Lord. Similarly, as Genesis makes clear, Jacob now knew the truth about *his* specialness to God.

The New Testament teaches the glorious truth that we, too— like Jacob, and like the apostles—have been chosen and given that *specialness*. We, who have accepted Jesus Christ as Lord and Saviour, are those who have been *chosen by God*. Scripture says:

For he chose us in him [Jesus] *before the creation of the world to be holy and blameless in his sight* [Ephesians 1:4a].

God has made a sovereign choice, and He has declared this in His word to be true of *you*. Our salvation is not a matter of our attractiveness to God, nor of our ability to earn it; it is a result of His choice. What the scripture tells us is that *we are chosen* and that, just as in the case of Jacob, we too have been chosen for a specific purpose,

For we are God's workmanship, created in Christ Jesus to do good

works, which God prepared in advance for us to do [Ephesians 2:10].

The Church is the body of Christ—a body in which every member has a part to play. When God made you new in Christ, He made you so that you might play your part in His body. He made you so that you might play your part in His grand plan. So He presents you with opportunities. It was Jacob's testimony, it was the disciples' testimony, and it is the testimony that God has given to each one of us.

We began by thinking about an election, which is a time of choice in our society. We now use the word 'election' in a very different sense, to describe our Christian calling. Our Christian 'election' is about *God choosing us* and issuing us with a mandate to serve under His authority alone. The Bible speaks of our having been elected by God, to keep us humble in our walk with Him, because it reminds us that it is by His grace, His free gift, that we are indeed His.

ACCOMPANIED BY GOD

Several years ago, whilst still at college, I heard a fellow student's testimony about a miracle that God had done in his life. He had become ill, and was taken to hospital. As part of the treatment for his condition, this man had to receive, every night, a very important but extremely painful injection. So painful was it that the student would become anxious—crying, and then screaming out with the pain. One night, when he felt that he could not take any more of this, Jesus came to his bed, just as the nurse was coming to give him yet another injection. The student said that Jesus sat on the side of his bed, held his hand, spoke reassuring words to him, and then, when the injection had been given, got up and left. The hospital staff were able to testify to the fact that this student had a visitor that night. That student's testimony was that *God was with him*. That was also Jacob's testimony, when he spoke to his uncle, Laban: it was that *God was with him*.

One of the fundamental attributes of God is that He is omnipresent—in all places. On the face of it, this is hard to understand. But what it means in this context is not that God is 'extended', as a material object would have to be if it were everywhere; rather, God is present as the creator and sustainer in existence of everything that is: things seen and unseen. What happened at the place 'formerly known as Luz' was that God was revealing to Jacob that He was with him in a very special way. The creator God, who was everywhere, was now manifesting His presence with Jacob.

It might be helpful if we identify some of the features of this presence. Firstly, it was a literal and not just some sort of figurative or metaphorical presence. Regarding the student in my story, it was later discovered that what had happened was that another student had been woken from sleep and was then led by the Lord to go to the hospital and sit with the patient. There had been, therefore, a figurative presence—not a literal one. For Jacob, on the other hand, it was a literal one.

Secondly, if the truth be told, God had always been with Jacob. From the moment of his birth to the moment of his death, God had been with him. The significance of his encounter with God at Bethel was that there he became aware of that presence, probably for the first time. As he says,

"Surely the Lord is in this place, and I was not aware of it" [28:16].

Thirdly, this spiritual presence would always be identified by a physical location. Repeatedly, in the life of Jacob, you will read that he returned to Bethel. Why? Because Bethel was the landmark for the occasion when his spiritual eyes were opened. It became his aid to faith. We all have them. For me it is Llanmadoc camp in the Gower. It was there that I came to faith; and there that meeting with God led to my making many of the important decisions in my life. To categorise these places, they are testimony locations, which remind us of encounters with God, encouraging us to go on seeking more from Him. If you have not visited one of yours lately, may I encourage you to have a day out soon, to do so.

Fourthly, do note how Jacob became aware of God's presence. [See v.12.] God spoke to Jacob through a dream. Revelation came through the supernatural. We should all open ourselves up to God speaking to us through pictures and dreams.

Fifthly, see how God introduces Himself; what it is that He says about Himself:

"...I am the Lord, the God of your father Abraham and the God of Isaac" [28:13b].

I was praying, recently, with a minister friend of mine. We were praying for growth in his spiritual life. One of the things we concentrated on was that God would give him a greater revelation of Himself. The most important thing about that minister's life and ministry is his understanding of God, an understanding at once both academic and experiential. That understanding determines everything. To Jacob, God disclosed that *He* was the one who was Lord—in control of it all; that *He* was God—who could do it all; and that He had a faithful relationship with Jacob's family. Similarly, He wants to disclose Himself to us.

Finally, one of the things which really impressed itself upon Jacob was God's promise that He would always be with him: *"I am with you and will watch over you wherever you go..."* [v.15]. It is instructive to consider this promise in the light of Psalm 23, in which the psalmist expresses faith in God's provision, experienced in all circumstances—even when walking through the valley of the shadow of death. Jacob knew now that *whatever* the situation he found himself in—and his life story tells us that he found himself dealing with many troubles and hazards—God would be with him. How exciting it must have been to Jacob to know that God was with him, and would be with him always.

Recall the experience of Shadrach, Meshach and Abednego, in the fiery furnace of King Nebuchadnezzar. In that furnace, which had been heated several times hotter than normal, not only were they not burned, but there, in the midst of the flames—in the middle of this testing of their faith, when their lives were at risk— God was with them, in an amazing way. For, as the king said,

"Weren't there three men that we tied up and threw into the fire?" ... *"Look! I see four men walking around in the fire, unbound and unharmed, and the fourth looks like a son of the gods."*
[See Daniel 3:24,25]

My wife and I found that an awesome thought at a time when we were going through one of the greatest challenges to our faith to date. We could identify with the position and condition of Shadrach, Meshach and Abednego. What a revelation; what a discovery, to know that there, in the midst of life, God is with us. That was Jacob's testimony, it is my testimony, and that is your testimony. For God is with you. The Scriptures give us the wonderful assurance that God has come and set up home in our hearts, from the moment we were born again. When you become a Christian, as Paul points out, Christ is *in* you. What that means is that *for us, today,* God is within us. We are not 'home alone'. We are not like lost children in a shopping centre. We are God's children, travelling through life with God as our companion.

As you read these words, you might be doing so in a home where your partner cares little for the Christian faith. Know this: that in your home, God is with you. Or again, tomorrow when you go to work, you might feel all alone. You are the only person there who believes in God. Know that God goes with you, and that He is there with you. This week, you might have to face an apparently insurmountable difficulty; maybe have to go into hospital or face some other unforeseen major event. Know that God is with you in the midst of it. You might not be able to see Him; you might not be able to feel Him—but He *is* there: 'Immanuel', God with us.

CHEERED ON BY GOD

I shall never forget the day my son represented his beaver group in a regional 'six a side' football competition in a tournament at our local leisure centre. His team did brilliantly. They were runners up, losing only one game.

That day was a special day for him, but it was also a special day for me. The reason for that was what I discovered about myself: I love my boy; I think the world of him. On that day, I discovered how much I was *for him*.

It was on the leisure centre balcony, with all the other participants' parents, that I felt an immense delight for our kids, and a desire for them to do well. Every time my son went for a ball, I cheered; every time he kicked the ball, I shouted him on; every time he stopped a player, I clapped. When his team scored, I danced with delight; when it was his turn to be left out, I was saddened for him. By the end of the two hour competition, I could hardly talk; I had lost my voice, and my body was aching from the tension of the games. I was *for* my boy, and I let everyone know it.

As Jacob walked off the holy ground of Bethel, he too would have known what it was like to have someone who was for him. Had God *chosen* him? Yes, he had. Was God *with* him? Yes, He was. But, more than that, now he knew that God was *for* him. Now the presence of God in his life was going to have real consequences. Whereas for my son, having me being for him meant my shouting and cheering and clapping and dancing with delight, for Jacob having God with him meant all that—joy in the heart of

God—and it was to mean much more, as well.

It meant, firstly, having God's leadership: *"...I will bring you back to this land..."* [v.15]. What exactly it would mean to have God's leadership in his life, Jacob could not have grasped at that time. To date, he had had no experience of it, but what he did know was that God had promised it to him. If we jump ahead to the end of his life, we discover that God honoured His word. Talking to Joseph about his days, Jacob speaks about the *"...God who has been my shepherd all my life..."* [48:15]. It was the Lord who had led him from Laban's place back home; it had been the Lord who had led him to Bethel again, and it was the Lord who, through circumstances, guided him to Egypt at the time of the famine. Whether through vision or prophecy, dream or picture, or through life's events—in all, God had honoured His word, and was leading him. Many people, with hindsight, see the hand of God guiding them. We are shown by God's word to Jacob that, for much of the time, he had been given grounds for such confidence. Scripture teaches that we can have that confidence too.

Secondly, having God as a supporter meant knowing God's protection. *"I am with you and will watch over you..."* [28:15]. Stories of deliverance from great perils are so encouraging. One of the great rescue stories of 1997 was the miraculous deliverance from his capsized boat of the British yachtsman Tony Bullimore. Through the speedy response of the Australian navy, Bullimore's life was saved.

As Jacob travelled through what may have seemed to him the uncharted and treacherous waters of life, there were many occasions when he could have found himself 'shipwrecked'. One specific incident is recorded in Genesis 31. Laban, discovering that Jacob had deserted him with his family and flocks, without a word, pursues him. The suggestion is that this is a hostile pursuit. Jacob is delivered through God warning Laban in a dream not to harm him. That action by God came from His being *for* Jacob. Scripture teaches that as God was for Jacob so He is for us. Like Jacob, we probably have little idea of just how much God's hand is upon us—guarding, preserving, protecting and saving us.

Thirdly, knowing God was on his side meant that Jacob was assured of God's commitment to finishing what He had started:

"...I will not leave you until I have done what I have promised you" [28:15].

St. Paul expresses the same truth in these words:

"...being confident of this, that he who began a good work in you will carry it on to completion..." [Philippians 1:6].

In Exodus Chapter 33, we are told of a moment in the life of Moses when he came to a crucial point of decision. The people of Israel had sinned with their golden calf. God's judgement had fallen upon them. However, after a period of forgiveness and reconciliation with God, His word came to Moses, saying that it was time to lead the people on. But he could not do so. How could he? He had seen the people at their worst: at the depths of degradation and sin. What was more, he could easily guess at the strength of the surrounding tribes. Contact with any of these would be disastrous. Moses knew that he could only go on *if God was for them.* If He were not, then their journey was pointless. We are told that God assured Moses of His presence and that He was for them.

The New Testament teaches that as it was for Moses, so it is for us; and as it was for Jacob, so it is for us. God is for us—on our side—and will bring us safely home. He wants to offer us His leadership; wants to give us His protection. The consequences of God being for us are truly amazing. Sometimes, when we contemplate our involvement in the work of God, we feel like the boy who could only offer five loaves and two fish—all we have, but so little when compared with the greatness of the need. The story tells us that what the boy had was more than enough for the crowd of five thousand. Why? Because the Lord was for him.

Why could Daniel be confident in the lions' den? Why could David face a giant? Why could every hero and heroine of faith do things which, to the natural eye, appear impossible? Is it not because they all had grasped that God was for them? As He was with them, so He will be with us, if we will have faith in Him.

When you pray, what is your understanding of God? One of the things Jesus identifies, again and again, is the nature of the One to whom we pray. We pray to the One who is for us—not one whose arm we have to twist up his back, nor one who wants the worst for us, but, rather, One who wants to delight us and who is better than any earthly father.

Let me ask you a personal question. Are you anxious about anything? In Matthew Chapter 5, Jesus gives us his understanding of the root of anxiety for most people. Do you know what it is? It is that they have a misunderstanding of God's opinion about them and His care of them. What Jacob was told, what Moses pleaded for, and what the New Testament declares is true for you and me, is that God is for us.

GOD WAS CHANGING HIM

In 2 Corinthians 3:18, we find the Apostle Paul, in the midst of his theological treatise on the new covenant that is ours, teaching the Corinthians one of the great principles of the Christian life:

And we, who with unveiled faces all reflect the Lord's glory, are being transformed into his likeness with ever-increasing glory, which comes from the Lord, who is the Spirit.

The truth he is communicating here is that those who contemplate the Lord are changed—that those who frequent the courts of heaven and gaze at Jesus, or who come into his presence and worship him or meditate upon him, will find that their lives begin to change as they are transformed into his likeness.

As Moses' appearance changed when he went up onto the mountain and his face shone with the glory of God, so it is for the Christian—the outcome of meeting with God is that we are changed. This reality—being changed through an encounter with God—can be seen in the life of Paul. Was it not his encounter with the resurrected Lord that changed the very course of his life? Similarly, in the life of Peter; and again, in the life of Zacchaeus, as with so many other people of whom we read in the Bible.

Such change on meeting God had certainly occurred for Jacob. In his talking to Laban, although it was only a relatively short period of time after his dramatic encounter with God, Jacob was able to play 'spot the difference' with his life.

What were those differences? Since meeting God, there had been a change in his attitude to Him, as well as toward his belongings, and toward his own life.

Prior to his encounter with God, there is no evidence that Jacob had given Him a great deal of thought. Jacob's only reference to God is, when speaking to his father, a false crediting of his success in hunting to God's involvement! Even here, this is ascribed to 'Isaac's God', not Jacob's. Yet immediately after his encounter with God there is a new reality—being *alive to* God's presence in his life. Admittedly, what we are shown may not be the most mature of reactions and attitudes, but they are, nonetheless, very lively ones. We learn that Jacob experiences *fear* towards God, then *wonder*, then, finally, *worship*.

When Jacob awoke from his sleep, he thought, "Surely the Lord is in this place, and I was not aware of it." He was afraid and said, "How awesome is this place! This is none other than the house of God; this is the gate of heaven" [Genesis 28:16–18].

As to the change in his attitude to his belongings, Jacob's early years had been marked by a 'me first' orientation. This attitude had prompted him to do the deceitful things that we have already noted. But after the meeting with God, Jacob had now become a man who begins to view belongings as a gift from God, and also as an area for the worship of God. We are told that Jacob will tithe all that he gets, in response to God's meeting with him:

"...and this stone that I have set up as a pillar will be God's house, and of all that you give me I will give you a tenth" [v.22].

Concerning his change of attitude about his own life, from the moment of Jacob's encounter with God at Bethel he decided *to live his life for God.* There was to be no more seeking to benefit himself, living in the good of his birthright, or special family blessing, no more just looking out for himself. From now on, Jacob will live for God:

"...so that I return safely to my father's house, then the Lord will be my God..." [v.21].

In the Epistle to the Galatians, the Apostle Paul uses the vivid imagery of taking off old garments, and putting on the new ones that are ours in Christ. As Jacob talked to his uncle, he would have been able to identify changes that have already taken place. Had they met again in years to come, he could no doubt have gone on to talk about a name change and the developing of a different walk.

The glorious thing is that all this is also true of our testimony, when we have encountered the living God for ourselves. We, too, are those who have been changed. What we could have been is not what we are. If you want to know what you could have been, have a look at your close relatives who do not know Christ and are not enjoying a relationship of faith and obedience, with the assurance of forgiveness of sins and eternal life.

Moreover, where we are now is not where we will finish! God has done many things in you: He has helped you to conquer sins and has brought new, good characteristics into your life; and He has begun to grow the 'fruit of the Spirit' in you—yet there is still so much more to come. One day we shall be like Him, and we will be enjoying His presence in the heavenly places, for ever. Astonishing as it might seem, that is the promise of God.

As a teenager, I sometimes wore a badge saying, 'Please be patient with me, God hasn't finished with me yet'. Such a plea is a glorious truth of our testimony. No, He has not finished with you or me yet—but He has started, and He will finish what He has started.

THE KING AND I

We have been thinking about the kind of testimony that Jacob could have given. He had a God who had *chosen* him, was *with* him, was *for* him and *changing* him. In the light of what we have looked at, I want to encourage you in the pursuit of God. Most of what Jacob knew about God came from his meetings with God. True, Jacob only had three such significant meetings during his life, but what significant meetings they were, and what a difference they caused. Thankfully, Jacob also knew the daily reality of God's presence; he knew the mountain top experience, the 'valley of the shadow of death' experience, and the daily grind experience—we will find that, in some measure, as we go through similar times.

We have seen how God transformed Jacob's life as he passed through this range of experiences, and how the Lord was there in the midst of all the troubles of life. Men and women of faith discover that they have to travel a long and costly road. Most give up along the way, but I encourage you to put your hiking boots on, fill up your backpack, and pursue God—that, like Jacob, you might meet with Him.

Since the God of Jacob is our God, the same God and Father of our Lord Jesus Christ, let me encourage you to live in the good of our God. He has chosen us. Live in that reality: appreciate that He has made a special choice—He has chosen you! God is with us—so open your heart, and let Christ dwell in you. God is for us—so let us stop projecting false images on to God. He is the Father who loves us, and who wants the best for us.

God wants to change us—so open up your life and invite Him in! Have an evening where you hand over the keys of all the rooms in your life to Him, and allow Him to walk around. I encourage you to take some time *this week* and reflect on how God has worked in your life over the years. Celebrate again how He called you.

Identify the times when you have known Him with you. Note the occasions when you have seen Him work for you. List the changes that He has carried out in you.

Finally, I encourage you to tell *your* faith story to someone else. You may be surprised at what a blessing it brings to that person to hear your testimony of the power of God at work in your life. Whether or not you are called to be an evangelist, every Christian is called to be a witness, and every Christian can tell his or her own story, and this really does help others, and lead them to seek their own encounter with Him.

There is a beautiful, true story of how one day, in the house of a Pharisee, a woman arrived who had previously had seven demons in her. Kneeling down before Jesus, she poured the costliest of perfumes over his feet. The room was filled with the fragrance of that perfume, and of the woman's worship. In breaking open that bottle, she was symbolically breaking open her life—and allowing all present to savour the aroma of freedom that Christ, who had released her from those demons, had given to her. We have testimonies which can do that for others, and which form part of our worship to Jesus. In pastoral groups, one to another and in church, take the opportunities afforded you to tell others about God in your life.

PRAYER

Heavenly Father, thank you that you are my God.
I ask you to reveal more of yourself to me.
I need you.
Show me what it means
to be chosen by you and accompanied by you;
to be cheered on by you and changed by you.
Cause my life to be an adventure of discovering you.

Four

REFINER'S FIRE

Genesis 29:1–31:55

During the prayer meeting before our evening service, Julia was
telling us of a picture that she felt the Lord had given her. The gist
of it was that there was someone in the room whom God was
refining. God wanted to give insight to that person: their feeling of
being isolated during this period was itself part of the refining;
and He was doing this in order that they might come out as 'gold'.

We are now thinking about a time in Jacob's life when that picture
would have been apt for him. What did it mean for Jacob, and
what does it mean for Christians, to be in that place of refining?
How does God refine us?

There are several things we need to understand. We never find
ourselves in such a position by chance. As we have seen, in
Ecclesiastes 3, Solomon describes contrasting seasons in our life.
Some are marked by things that seem to us positive and
beneficial—depicted as 'planting', 'building up', 'gaining'.... Other
seasons seem so destructive and hard—described as 'breaking-
down', 'mourning', 'throwing away'.... Yet, ultimately, God is
involved in both.

The episode of refining which we are considering happened
whilst Jacob was at the home of Laban, his uncle. As we know, he
was there because of his sin of deceit towards his father and

brother, following his subsequent flight. (Genesis 28:5). However, the way in which this situation came about should not be taken to mean that this difficult time in Jacob's life arose solely from his personal sin. As we see at so many other points in Scripture, God is able to use all situations for His own ends. (See, for example, Romans 8:28, where it is affirmed that He works for the good of those who love Him and are called according to His purpose.) God was working providentially through events. *The refining process was not happening by chance.* This becomes apparent in the way God allowed life to become difficult for Jacob.

We note that the temperature and characteristics of the refining 'furnace', are of specific design. It is the same for us. In John 15, Jesus tells us that the Father is like a gardener who prunes the vine. As a skilled and knowledgeable gardener, He knows *how* to cut and *when* to cut, He knows *what* to cut and *how deep* to cut. So, when we find ourselves in the fiery furnace, we do so in a personally designed environment.

The purpose of refining is primarily that we might be broken, bringing us to the end of self-dependency—to the point at which we realise that we have nothing in our hands to offer Him. We acknowledge that we are, in the words of Paul, "the worst of sinners" [1Tim.1:16]. The seed which has fallen on the ground begins to die, so that it can grow in a new way.

The breaking of the self occurs in order that we might be remoulded. One day, when my wife was emptying the dishwasher and putting the cups and glasses away, the cupboard where we kept them fell off the wall. Almost every cup and glass we owned was ruined, and all the smashed bits had to be thrown away. God's breaking of us is unlike this. He will not discard us—unlike glassware which had been rendered useless and fit only for the bin. When He breaks us, He does so in order that He might then remould, not destroy. Before that remoulding happens, there is normally a struggle, as the dross—rebellion, stubbornness and self-sufficiency—begin to surface. Only as these are dealt with are we brought to self-surrender, when at last we bow the knee and say, "not my will, but yours, be done".

Consider the emotions we experience during such a difficult time. We feel out of control, out of our depth, and uncomfortable. We may feel irritated and anxious, touchy about everything and need to be 'in the right' about things. There can be a deep vulnerability. One gets a severe case of 'spiritual pre-moulding tension'!

It is important that we understand that, usually, there is a choice in this refining process: we can choose to go with it, or we can reject it. This is no easy road. At times you feel as if you are being beaten up by thugs; you come to the point where you plead with them to stop. Being refined is not something that you glory in or shout about, but, rather, something sacred and personal.

Such refining takes a long time. God placed Jacob in this season for twenty years. We live in a 'microwave' age, when people expect things immediately, yet, with God, it simply does not work like that. Jacob was heated up repeatedly, and he was hammered repeatedly.

Finally, observe that God used a whole host of means to refine Jacob. He used people (particularly Laban, God's 'grit' in Jacob's eye), and He used crushing personal circumstances. For us He might use illness, unemployment, personal fears, difficult neighbours, relatives, problems in the family, or, indeed, almost any adverse situation.

GOD'S COMMITMENT TO CHANGING US
A minister was asked to conduct the wedding of a parishioner's daughter. It was a great honour for the man, as the family were well known and many very important people from the area would be present. The preparations for the wedding had gone well, except for the fact that the daughter, who was not accustomed to church, was worried that she would not remember her words. The vicar, keen for everything to run smoothly, went to see the girl the night before the wedding. To calm her down, he talked her through her part the next day. "When you come into the church, the music will play and you will walk down the aisle. Then you will come to the altar. When you get to the altar, you will reach your fiancé; then you will turn to him." He reinforced the order of things: "Walk down the aisle; come to the altar; turn to him." Next day, all went smoothly at the wedding. The bride played her part well—except for one thing: she was heard to mutter repeatedly, as she walked down the aisle, "I'll alter him"! Similarly, when God met with Jacob at Bethel, some days before he came to Laban's house, in the midst of making him the great declarations and promises, it was as though God was declaring, 'I'll alter him'.

God committed Himself to Jacob, but He was also committed to changing him. What we will see from this episode in Jacob's life is how He did just that. As we look at what God did in Jacob's life, we should realise that this is His commitment to us, too. God longs to advance us in His school, to groom us and to better us.

MARRIAGE DIFFICULTIES [Genesis 29:14–30]
After seven years of estrangement, my friend was reunited with his wife. They had been working up to it for some time, only eventually carrying it through when counselling had helped them identify and face most of the issues. Those seven years have been difficult, to say the least. Being told by his wife that she hated him, and that she never wanted to live with him, and having to say goodbye to their children as she walked out of their home, hurt immensely. They were tough years, too, in that my friend decided to take a biblical attitude to his marriage, committing himself to working through his trouble. His friends would be able to tell you that the consequence of this decision is that he has been broken, and broken again. Layers have been peeled and peeled away, until at times you might have wondered whether there was anything left. He has had to face the sort of issues none of us wants to face. It is no exaggeration to say that his marriage has been hell. For this man there has been a continual challenge to be forgiving and patient.

When Jacob married (See Genesis Chapter 29), in all probability he had no idea that the years ahead were going to be so turbulent. For seven years he had courted and wooed his bride. He had worked to pay the 'bride price' for her. His belief was probably that they would live 'happily ever after'. What happened on the first morning of his honeymoon was that Jacob made the same discovery as the character in *Four Weddings and a Funeral* who (nearly) married the wrong girl. Sadly for Jacob, it was too late. Instead of marrying Rachel, Jacob had woken up to find that he had married Leah, her older and less attractive sister. The deceiver had himself been deceived, by his father-in-law. A sub heading for this chapter could easily have been, 'How to be a difficult in-law'. The measure of deception Jacob had used towards his own brother Esau was now pressed down and running over—and coming back to him. We are told that Laban had a reason for his behaviour: it was the custom for the elder daughter to be married first. Laban told Jacob that he was not to worry, for if he agreed to work for another seven year stretch, then he could marry Rachel. What a formula for trouble! Despite Laban's reassurance, Jacob was broken by his discovery. In a later period, the marriage of two sisters to one man was outlawed in Israel, and the wisdom of that prohibition (in Leviticus) is amply illustrated by this incident. Jacob's marriage problems were further compounded by the fact that each of the sisters decided she wanted to be the prominent one. Again and again, these women are to be found squabbling over their husband. Proverbs tells us that a nagging wife is like a dripping tap. What a powerful image: dripping water was allegedly one of the most successful interrogation methods of the Japanese army for wearing a man down. Poor old Jacob! His pain was intensified by the fact that he found that he had a heart full of love for Rachel, but no love for Leah—something of which Leah was acutely aware, of course, and which is reflected in the naming of her children.

Leah became pregnant and gave birth to a son. She named him Reuben, for she said, "It is because the Lord has seen my misery. Surely my husband will love me now."

She conceived again, and when she gave birth to a son she said, "Because the Lord heard that I am not loved, he gave me this one too." So she named him Simeon.

Again she conceived, and when she gave birth to a son she said, "Now at last my husband will become attached to me, because I have borne him three sons." So he was named Levi.

[Genesis 29:32–34]

As I think of my friend who has now been reconciled with his wife, I know that, in the process of going through all he has endured, he has become a better man. There is, in him, a frightening honesty but—more than that—he has come to a point where he can distinguish what is important from what is just superficial. Many of his friends are now awed by his company. Whether such wisdom was the fruit of experience in Jacob's life, we cannot tell. All we know is that it was hoped for. God had determined to refine His chosen one, and, for Jacob, his marriage was one of the areas he used. It may be the same with us.

CHILD BEARING PROBLEMS [Genesis 29–30]
Why some people can have children and why others cannot is a mystery. For many who cannot, it is also a nightmare scenario. We have several sets of friends who are unable to bear children. They may be the best possible prospective parents. They may try

all the treatment modern science has made available, yet they still cannot conceive. This reality has a number of consequences for our friends. One couple decided to foster, another to adopt, while another simply decided to live as a childless couple. Heartbreak has overshadowed some of their lives, though most of them hide it well. But it is there nonetheless, and occasionally you see it— maybe on Mothers' Day, Fathers' Day, their own birthday, or when one of their friends gives birth. Sometimes the heartbreak is so deep that the marriage collapses.

Infertility was one of the situations God used in Jacob's marriage, to refine the man. Jacob had to deal with a barren wife. We are told that Rachel was unable to have children: *"...but Rachel was barren"* [29:31b]. The situation was complicated by the remarkable fertility of Jacob's other wife, Leah. So desperate was Rachel that she decided to try an old wives' tale which could have been the precursor of today's IVF treatment. Supposedly, mandrake plants were viewed as being able to stimulate reproduction. We are told that she was prepared to pay highly for them:

During wheat harvest, Reuben went out into the fields and found some mandrake plants, which he brought to his mother Leah. Rachel said to Leah, "Please give me some of your son's mandrakes."

But she said to her, "Wasn't it enough that you took away my husband? Will you take my son's mandrakes too?"

"Very well," Rachel said, "He can sleep with you tonight in return for your son's mandrakes." So when Jacob came in from the fields that evening, Leah went out to meet him. "You must sleep with me," she said. "I have hired you with my son's mandrakes." So he slept with her that night. [30:14–16.]

Although we are given only a glimpse, we are told that such a situation of barrenness was a cause of tension for Rachel, and between Rachel and Jacob. It seems that it sparked many an argument.

When Rachel saw that she was not bearing Jacob any children, she became jealous of her sister. So she said to Jacob, "Give me children, or I'll die!"

Jacob became angry with her and said, "Am I in the place of God, who has kept you from having children?" [30:1–2]

Rachel finally bore Jacob children. Yet the significant thing is that first there had to be a *moulding* of both the man and his wife— as it had been for Rebekah and for Sarah (her husband's mother and grandmother), so it was now for Rachel. Such was the second way that God moulded Jacob; it is one way that He may be using to mould us. For some, though, as I have already commented, such moulding does not conclude with a child being born. For them, the test of trust continues.

WORK HASSLES [Genesis 30:25–43]
For perhaps forty eight weeks of the year, over a period of forty years, more or less, you can expect to have to work! Some people are blessed in doing work they enjoy. I have a friend who hates what he does: his job depresses him. Sadly, try as he may, he just cannot get another job. You may be in a good job, doing what you think is valuable, yet many others would not enjoy your work, whilst others again might look enviously at your employment. You might be in the happy situation of working with friendly people, and find going to work a pleasure. Once I worked in Edinburgh with a great team of people; they were a joy to be with. You may be well-paid in comparison with others—even if your earnings are not as much as you want, nor what you feel you are worth. But whatever your position at work, there is something you can be sure of: there will be times when you experience problems in that arena of life—maybe because you are a Christian, or for many other reasons.

Jacob's life was dogged by difficulty at work. Unhappily for him, it turned out to be a difficulty he could not leave there. After all, Jacob had married the boss's daughters! His father-in-law repeatedly cheated him out of fair wages:

"You know that I've worked for your father with all my strength, yet your father has cheated me by changing my wages ten times."
[31:6–7]

Furthermore, his father-in-law was reluctant to let him move on. Laban even used his delving into the forbidden area of divination to furnish putative evidence of the wrongs of such a move. (See 30:25–28.) We do not know why Jacob wanted to go at that point. Maybe it was because now, with a family, he was ready to go and receive his father's flocks, which would be his by inheritance. Perhaps he thought the grass of the other place was greener. Whatever the reason, Jacob found himself locked in a fast track to nowhere. Working for his father-in-law also meant he would have been in a subordinate role, unable to develop his own livelihood properly, and this state of affairs may well have been irksome for him. Unable to leave, and having spent so much time nurturing his father-in-law's flocks, Jacob had been unable to develop his own herd. Admittedly, this was to change, but there were further problems when it did:

"The little you had before I came has increased greatly, and the Lord has blessed you wherever I have been. But now, when may I do something for my own household?" [Genesis 30:30]

Imagine being locked into such a dead end situation, with no hope of getting free: trapped like a rat. This was Jacob's lot for a considerable portion of his life, and it was this that God used to refine him. It may be your work situation which God is using to refine you!

HAVING TO MOVE ON [Genesis 31:1–55]
In 1995, my wife and I felt it was time to leave a pastorate. I had been pastor of the church for only fourteen months when we concluded that it was time to move on. In coming to a decision there were many things we had to work through; many questions that needed answering. Why were we leaving? Was God really calling us on? What would happen to the church, once we left? As to ourselves and our children, where would we go? Where would we live? Which school would our children attend? How would we live? If I resigned, how would I find the money to manage? Surely God was not calling me to be unemployed, was He? As we contemplated leaving, we had to face our fears and, by faith, walk in obedience.

Jacob had to face a situation of similarly grave uncertainty. He, too, felt that it was time to move on. Why? There were many reasons. It was true that Laban's attitude toward him had changed. Moreover, the attitude of Laban's sons had changed towards Jacob, and they were becoming increasingly jealous. But, above all, God was calling him to move.

Jacob heard that Laban's sons were saying, "Jacob has taken

everything our father owned and has gained all this wealth from what belonged to our father." And Jacob noticed that Laban's attitude toward him was not what it had been.
Then the Lord said to Jacob, "Go back to the land of your fathers and to your relatives, and I will be with you" [31:1–3].

When should he go? We are told that Jacob consulted his wives, and that they were in agreement. We do not know how long he waited until he packed. Some suggest that he had the word for a long time before he moved on it. If he did, that was a dangerous place to be. (If God has called us on, we should go—now). How should they leave? That was the crucial one. It is a crucial one for all of us. If God calls us to move on, it is important that we also discover the way that we should do that. Jacob decided to sneak away:

Moreover, Jacob deceived Laban the Aramean by not telling him he was running away. So he fled with all he had, and crossing the River, he headed for the hill country of Gilead [31:20].

There is much speculation about that decision. Some suggest it was a lack of faith: if God had called him to leave, then he should have left in full view of Laban and his family. Other commentators, however, believe that it was a sign of great wisdom. Jacob had attempted to leave before, and Laban was having none of it. If he tried to do it again, he could be sure that Laban would try to stop him. In leaving, Jacob had to face his fears over Laban and the probability that, even if he did sneak away, Laban was sure to catch him. The story is that Laban did catch him.

OUR PLACE IN THE 'FURNACE'
In such a situation as Jacob's, it is very easy to play safe. We have several friends who have not moved with God when He called them on. We read their newsletters and see that they are still struggling to find God's path for their lives. They may have lost the path several years ago, and are unwilling to repent of that and be open to walking it again. Jacob did respond to God's prompting. The struggle that went with his response was a further way God used to refine Jacob.
In this chapter we have been looking at the making of a man of God. Clearly, it is not an easy path to tread. Pruning is painful.

Becoming 'downwardly mobile' is both tough in itself and contrary to the values of an acquisitive modern society—yet it is sometimes a consequence of obedience to the call of God on your life.

If you find yourself in the place of testing, take heart! Remember that God is not going to give up on you when you fail. As we go through these difficult times in our lives, we can be assured that God will bring us through them. He will come to our aid and give us the strength to finish the course. He is going to be there with you. The Bible says that God only disciplines those He loves, His sons: this is part of being in the family, belonging to Christ.

For those who respond, a crown of gold awaits them. On the occasions when Jacob submitted, he emerged the better for having come through the experience.

For me, the place of refining is the birthplace of songs. Use songs that speak *to* God, as well as those that declare the truth *about* Him; use psalms to praise God, too. Open yourself up to the Holy Spirit: ask Him to touch you and to fill you afresh.

Be joyful always; pray continually; Give thanks in all circumstances [1 Thess. 5:16]. Praise Him, even as you experience the troubles of life. The faithful who endure will be greatly rewarded—so go on believing; go on trusting; and pray without ceasing.

PRAYER

Heavenly Father, as you refine me, let me know your grace daily.
My heart's desire is to be like Jesus. Make me like him.
My God, I find it very easy to run away from the furnace—
Hold me in your grip,
and do that work in me which needs to be done.

Five

STEPS TO RECONCILIATION

Genesis 32–33

In October 1985, my dad died. As a family, we had known that all was not well with him, but when it finally happened we were all taken by surprise. A heart attack in the middle of the afternoon had brought his relatively short life to an end. When, on that dark Wednesday evening, I was called out of class at theological college, and told that he had passed away, I was devastated, as you can imagine. The journey home, in my friend's van, saw me pass through a variety of emotions. For many years before his death there had been enmity in our relationship. We just could not agree. The primary cause of this jarring had been my decision to give up my job and go into full-time Christian work. Not a believer himself, he saw as reckless my resignation from my job and this foolish step into the unknown and uncertainty. His concern for me expressed itself in anger at me; my response was a stubborn refusal to hear what he had to say and refusal to explain my reasons. Inevitably, all this led to the breakdown of our relationship. Although that had been the state of things between us for several years, he died with us, at peace. On the Saturday prior to his death, I had come home from college for a long weekend, and impulsively decided to call in and see him. What I found was a man who had been broken by his recent illnesses, and who was not only pleased to see his son but was now open to restoring our relationship. Although it was only a brief time together, there were tears and hugs as we expressed our love for each other. Thank God for that weekend.

We move now to the time in Jacob's life when he passed through a similarly poignant and significant period, when the issue of reconciliation was high on the agenda. For twenty years there had been enmity between Jacob and Esau. As we have followed some of the events of Jacob's life, we have noticed the enmity he provoked when he deceived his brother out of the special family blessing. But now it was time for that division to be healed. In Paddan Aram, God had brought Jacob to the point at which he was ready to go home. As he obeyed, it seems that one of the things that God laid heavily on his heart was the task of bringing about that restoration of fellowship with his brother.

Let us consider the practical and spiritual steps which Jacob took, as he sought and, finally, achieved that reconciliation. There are various ways in which broken relationships can be repaired, but Jacob's way helps us to understand the direction we should be going in, for it takes us to the core of the matter, providing an excellent starting point.

First, though, a few thoughts about harmonious relationships—and their absence. Although, in the case of Jacob and Esau, we are looking at the coming together of two individuals from the same family, the steps we will identify are just as relevant to the reconciliation of individuals in the church family. Remember that disharmony has been a common enough feature of the corporate life of Christians from the outset. The New Testament provides ample evidence that this was the case in the early church. Believers fell out with each other. We have Paul falling out with Barnabas; we have Paul falling out with Peter; we have Paul falling out with the church at Corinth, and we have Paul falling out with the Judaizers. In the church at Philippi we have Euodia falling out with Syntyche. In the mother church in Jerusalem, we have the Hellenistic Christians falling out with the orthodox Christians, as it was felt that the widows in the Hellenistic section were not being treated fairly. The divisions certainly did not end there. To recognize the reality of such divisions in the body of Christ is neither to condemn nor condone them with the benefit of hindsight. To do either would be absurd. The point is simply that, whilst the believers in the church were endowed with the

Holy Spirit, they also continued to battle against the 'flesh'. By the term 'flesh' we mean all those things in us which have not yet come into complete obedience to God's perfect law of love. Consequently, disharmony of one sort or another should never surprise us.

What are we to do about it? The mandate of Scripture—the command of the Lord—is that disciples of Jesus should love one another. (See John 17). We are to seek reconciliation on this basis. That does not mean that we have gooey feelings for one another, but rather that when there are times of strain, tension, dislike or disharmony between us, we commit ourselves to working through to a state of peace, on the basis of real concern for the good of others, yet never compromising revealed truth. That is what Jesus prayed for—that they might be one, even as the Father and he are one.

We see such skirmishes in all kinds of Christian settings. To those who may be bystanders as the battle rages, the biblical principle of love requires that you be a 'guerilla for peace'. You are not a neutral observer, because you are part of the same body: do everything you can to foster reconciliation between your Christian brothers and sisters. There are many things in the church and in Christendom that have the potential to divide: new spiritual movements, women in ministry, the direction of the church, as well as simple personality clashes.

Of course, divisions in the world are always to be expected. Jesus warned his disciples about the wars which were yet to take place. Divisions for the sake of the gospel arise from time to time, when men who cannot see the truth begin to encounter it. Jesus also warned that a person's response to him could result in family disharmony, and sometimes that has to be borne for his sake. It is our calling to be peacemakers wherever we can, working for peace and the healing of damaging divisions wherever we find them, in both open and private ways (for 'blessed are the peacemakers').

As we think about reconciliation, we have to address the great issues of repentance, confession and forgiveness. We move into an area that has the potential to release an awful lot of hurt and pain. So it is important, then, that we are wise. We need to think before we speak; we need to think before we act; and being open to the Holy Spirit is no guarantee that Christians always act and speak wisely! Born again, Spirit-filled believers do sometimes get things wrong; supposed guidance is not always adequately tested;

there is sometimes much subjectivity, and charges of emotionalism are not always entirely unjustified. So we proceed with caution.

In obedience to Jesus' commands in Mark 11:25 and Matthew 5:23, we will sometimes see a real need to go and restore a broken down relationship, before 'offering our gift at the altar'. Those scriptures are standing instructions to disciples always to be ready to put matters right. In addition, sometimes the Holy Spirit will show us specifically that this is necessary and timely. So how do we set about it? How did Jacob do it?

TAKE THE INITIATIVE [Genesis 32:1–3]

Bill Hybels, pastor of one of the largest churches in America, writes of how a fellow Pastor in one of the local churches was publicly criticising him and his wife. Hybels tells how, out of jealousy or envy, or perhaps because he had been given one side of a juicy bit of gossip, this man was demeaning them—both from his pulpit, and in private. Bill writes of the time they decided to do something about it. Instead of letting the situation run, instead of just sweeping it under the carpet, one day he and his wife went to speak to the man, in his office. They decided to take the initiative and open up the possibility of reconciliation.

That is what Jacob did: he took the initiative.

Jacob sent messengers ahead of him to his brother Esau in the land of Seir, the country of Edom. He instructed them: "This is what you are to say to my master Esau: 'Your servant Jacob says, I have been staying with Laban and have remained there till now. I have cattle and donkeys, sheep and goats, menservants and maidservants. Now I am sending this message to my lord, that I may find favour in your eyes'" [Genesis 32:1–5].

To take the initiative, Jacob had to go out of his way, both geographically and psychologically. It would have been natural to enter Canaan by the north, but instead he entered it by the south, nearer to his brother. It would not be unreasonable to suppose that Jacob's preference would have been to sneak back into Canaan in a way that would have avoided the risk of an encounter with the formerly enraged Esau.

Note the means by which Jacob took the initiative. He sent a concise message to his brother, delivered by one of his servants. See the wisdom here. He does not burst in on his brother, but begins to prepare the ground. He is also wise enough to do it through another, so that his face does not evoke an irrational response.

Note also that Jacob initiated this attempt to bond again with his brother in an attitude of submission, and with the purpose of peace. Jacob was not looking for another fight, and he told Esau as much. Moreover, he was coming in the knowledge that he would be placing himself at the mercy of his brother. Now, admittedly, it took Jacob twenty years to get to that point, but get there he did.

If God is challenging you over a breakdown in one of your relationships, let me encourage you to follow Jacob's example and take the initiative to bring about reconciliation. It might mean that you have to go out of *your* way, both geographically and psychologically but, as this scripture teaches us, it is the right way to go. As you go, remember to go wisely. Follow Jacob's example and prepare the person before attempting to bring about reconciliation. If necessary, you can write first, or make contact through a friend, or (taking the advice of Matthew 18) take someone else along, too.

Whether you see yourself as the wronged, innocent person or as the more guilty party, you are the one seeking to initiate reconciliation: do so in an attitude of submission; let it be known that you are making contact for this reason. Of course, if someone else, like Jacob, moves towards you with a view to reconciling some difference between you, do appreciate the distance that this person has travelled; have mercy on them, and be sure to help the process along by your attitude.

KNOW YOUR GOAL [Genesis 32:5]
When I was a youth worker, someone wrote a letter to the church elders, which criticised the way I had handled a youth service. It was obvious to those exercising oversight that the letter was but the 'tip of the iceberg' as far as the complainant was concerned. Throughout recent years, this person had struggled with the changes that the evangelical minister had sought to bring about in the church. There had been a struggle with the worship, the style of preaching, and with the whole direction of the church. What this person saw as my erroneous conducting of the service caused an inward boiling to spill over. On behalf of the elders, the steering group sought to reconcile the situation. They wrote to this person, accepting that whilst I could have done better, they

affirmed their support of me. They also offered to meet with the aggrieved individual, if it were felt that that would be beneficial. They decided to take that particular line, in order to stimulate a situation where we would be at peace with one another; so that we might be able to look one another in the face. They were keen to do what they could to ensure that no faction should emerge in the church. Perhaps you have seen one of those sad situations: one sits over here, and another over there; another doesn't go to this or that house group because so and so goes there, and they fell out with so and so, who is my friend. How easily all that can start.

Making contact with his brother, Jacob tells Esau that his goal is to find favour in his eyes. Roughly translated, this meant that they might be able to look into each other's eyes and not find hostility, resentment or bitterness there. Jacob is looking for an open, wholesome relationship with his brother. They might not like each other, but they would love each other. Jacob is in the wrong. He knows that. He is aware that he has sinned against his brother, and that his brother has suffered as a result. Jacob's goal is that that sin of his might be covered and dealt with. That is why, in this situation, he takes the opportunity to imply his repentance.

Whether or not you are the 'guilty party', we should take such an attitude, with such a goal in view. Jesus said that through the love we Christians have one for another, the world will know that we are his disciples. To love one another means to be committed to working through to a state of fellowship with people with whom we have fallen out. This is what we see Jacob doing with his brother Esau.

FACE YOUR FEARS [Genesis 32:7–8]

In great fear and distress Jacob divided the people who were with him into two groups, and the flocks and herds and camels as well. He thought, "If Esau comes and attacks one group, the group that is left may escape" [Genesis 32:7].

Clearly, Jacob was afraid for his life. Perhaps he feared rejection. So frightened was he, that he divided his camp. When we work to restore broken relationships, including those occasions when we are to blame, we need to be aware that we, too, will have to face our fears, courageously doing what is right. As we do so, we should take heart, for God is going to be with us as we walk the path of reconciliation. As Jacob was reconciled with Esau, he discovered that God was with him, for the meeting was blessed.

Remember that fear is the opposite of faith, and when a course of action is clearly required from us as a matter of obedience to the command of God, we need not fear anything or anyone. If we ask Him for wisdom as to how to deal with the situation, He will show us the way through it, so that under the guidance of the Holy Spirit we will be helped to find the right words and the right approach.

PRAY YOUR PRAYERS [Genesis 32:9–12]
In John 17, we are given the prayer that Jesus prayed the night before he was crucified, often referred to as his 'high priestly' prayer. Jesus knows then that his time on earth is nearly over. He knows that from tomorrow, in many senses, his disciples are going to be left on their own. He appreciates the scope of the mission that is theirs, and the many pitfalls they could fall into. So, on the eve of his death, he gives himself to prayer for them.

One of the things Jesus prays for is the unity of the people he will leave behind. As Paul would later pray on the beach at Miletus, for the Ephesian elders, so Jesus prays that his followers would be marked by a oneness, which would speak volumes to the world.

By his prayer, Jesus demonstrated and taught the importance of prayer in the context of reconciled relationships. Paul had learnt this lesson. So, evidently, had Jacob on this, the first occasion that we read of him spontaneously praying. Consider the characteristics of his prayer in 32:9–12. That he was now rooted in the great purposes of God we see in v.12; that he is aware of the promises of God to him, in vv. 9–10; pleading that, as he seeks to fulfil God's leading and reconcile with his brother, God would protect him, in v.11. We see that this was a prayer God answered, and we would be wise to follow Jacob's example.

When I was in a prayer meeting once, after a time of waiting on the Lord, one of the people asked if we could pray for two of the leaders. He did not know that the two leaders in question were in the downward spiral of disharmony. God had laid it on that young Christian's heart to pray for those men. I believe he laid it on Paul's heart, and on Jacob's heart to seek unity by praying. Above all, we know that it was the Father's will, perfectly expressed in that prayer of Jesus. Disunity is as much a result of enemy activity in the course of spiritual warfare as it is of the sinful will. What is needed is both prayer to open up the way, and an act of repentance. Admittedly, Jacob prayed from a position of fear. To pursue reconciliation, we need to pray. Pray for wisdom. Pray for a good reception by the other person. Pray for harmony.

PLAN THE MOMENT [Genesis 32:12–20]
John and his wife had been the leaders of the church youth group. Under his leadership it had gone fairly well; people attending were happy with it. On my being appointed to the leadership, the minister and the group responsible had asked that I join them and start leading it. John and his wife decided that they would stay in the group and help with the task. After a while, it became obvious that John was not happy with the direction that the group was taking. More than that, he was happy neither with my leadership of the group nor with me. Although not apparent to the group, it was obvious to me that our openness with each other was disappearing. There was no longer harmony.

What would you do in such a situation? After praying, Sarah and I decided to invite John and his wife around for supper, to have a pleasant evening with them and to address the issue that was provoking this 'spiritual arthritis', this grinding of the joints. What was the key which would solve the problem? Two things helped move us forward. I spent some time telling John how much I appreciated all the work he had done with the youth group, and how his involvement was so valuable now. The other thing I did was to ask him what he thought I was saying about the direction and future of the group. My plan, conceived in prayer, worked a treat. As a result of our evening together, we were in a place of harmony. John and his wife have remained our friends for many years. The point about that evening's success is that I had the right plan for the occasion. Yes, I had prayed, but I had also thought and prepared a way which would ease the re-establishment of harmony.

When Jacob came to meet Esau, he came armed with a plan, as well. This was not going to be a spur of the moment thing—'stand up and confess your sin, and then expect reconciliation'. Appreciating the seriousness of the moment, Jacob prepared himself for it. He determined to prepare Esau, through the giving of a gift. What made matters worse for Jacob was his belief that

Esau would not at first be receptive to his invitation to reconcile. That Esau was coming with four hundred men provided ample evidence that he was determined to make war. If that was the case, then we can appreciate the place and importance of that plan. Was it manipulative? No— it was wisdom at work. It was graciousness at work: humility. Had Esau wished, he could have ignored it. If he were even slightly open to the notion of reconciliation, it would win him over. It did.

This idea of preparing for the moment of reconciliation is something we find the apostle Paul doing. When it came time for Paul to send the now converted runaway slave Onesimus to his owner, Philemon, Paul took the time to prepare for that return. He wrote that classic of letters, Philemon, a guide to diplomacy and tact. That Paul prepared for the return of Onesimus probably saved the slave's life. Such attention to detail, and commitment to diplomacy, should mark our efforts in the restoration of our relationships.

DO THE DEED [Genesis 33:1–11]
It is all well and good talking about reconciliation, talking about initiating it, praying about it, planning it. But there comes a point when you have to actually get on and do it; when you get together, sit down and talk the issue out, or commit yourselves again to each other. That is what we find Jacob doing next. All the planning and praying is finished. Esau has arrived, and it is time to do the deed. Superficially, it might look as though Esau's arrival takes Jacob by surprise. But that is not the case. He is ready for this moment.

See how there is a one-on-one encounter. On seeing Esau arrive, Jacob goes out and stands in front of his family. The message is clear: those not involved should stay out of it.

See how Jacob expresses his contrition. As Esau approaches, he bows down. When he speaks to him, it is with honest flattery: *"For to see your face is like seeing the face of God, now that you have received me favourably"* [33:10b]. Of course it was. To some extent there has already been a confession of sin, signified in the way that Jacob has asked Esau to look with favour in his eyes.

See Esau expressing forgiveness: *But Esau ran to meet Jacob and embraced him; he threw his arms around his neck and kissed him. And they wept"* [33:4]. This was a rather emotional time with tears, hugs and kisses. Is there, perhaps, some echo of this reconciliation in the Gospel account of the father's reception of the prodigal son?

Remember that Jacob had no guarantee of the response he would get from Esau. He had hoped and prayed, planned and then 'gone for it', and the time had now come. He and his brother are one again. What a marvellous moment of reconciliation, and what an example here for young Joseph, in later life.

Observe that Jacob does not settle until he has the assurance of forgiveness. His brother has responded to his contrition, but he must know for sure that they are at peace. Esau must accept his gifts. He presses him until it is done. As he says, it is his sign that he has found favour in his brother's eyes.

Finally, see the rebirth of fellowship. There is the introduction of family members, of children to their uncle, and of wives to their brother-in-law.

Jacob had worked for a positive, deliberate and explicit reconciliation, and he had got it. Wonderful, wasn't it? So it can sometimes be for us, when reconciliation is needed. Such an encounter may be charged with emotion, but there is spiritual business to be done, and it is important that it is done right. There is a confession to be made, forgiveness to be given, and the re-kindling of fellowship to begin. Such moments are sacred. When we are involved in an act of reconciliation, we gain our inspiration and motivation from what Jesus taught, and from his unique, saving death on Calvary. Special moments of reconciliation should not be passed over lightly or quickly. When divided Christians are reconciled, it can sometimes be appropriate to move into prayer together, or the breaking of bread.

But what if the person with whom you need reconciliation will not respond? Just leave the offer of reconciliation on the table, with the invitation that, whenever they might want to take it up, you will be ready. Yes, that means there is no closure on this issue and yes there is pain and heartache, but you will know that you have obeyed the great command to love. Jesus shares the pain of rejection that you may feel. He knew what it was to feel rejection, yet he showed us how to go on loving even as the nails were driven in.

What if the person with whom there was enmity has died? Do not address the deceased. To do so is not permitted by God. Simply commit the matter to Him. Express your repentance for your part in the breakdown to the Lord; then be assured of forgiveness. Do not go on in remorse and regret for the missed opportunities of the past. God desires that you should now have life abundantly, and experience His healing grace.

WORK IT OUT WISELY [Genesis 33:12–20]
After Jacob and Esau had done their making up, Esau invited Jacob to accompany him to his home. Since they were living as brothers again, Esau had assumed that they would go home together. Jacob, it seems, had other ideas: he would not be able to travel at the same speed as Esau and his men; he had children and cattle and they would slow him down. Jacob's thought was that Esau should proceed and he would follow slowly.

Esau offers to leave some of his men to go with him. Again, Jacob is reported to have declined. Why leave any men? There was no need. Esau could go on. Jacob would join him later.

In each step one takes in the process of securing unity, it is necessary to walk by the light of God's wisdom. This remains as true, if not more so, after the act of reconciliation has taken place. Following his encounter with Esau, Jacob then needed and wanted some space apart from him, and to have some rest time for himself. He went off to worship, carrying on with his God given call to settle back in the Promised Land.

Are we to conclude, then, that Jacob had only been half-hearted in his reconciliation with his brother, using it perhaps for his own end? Certainly not: this was wisdom in operation. It takes time to restore in practice that which has only recently been restored spiritually and in principle. To engage in the process of reconciliation is to engage in a very stressful and tiring exercise. Once our part in it has been carried out, there is a need to take time for rest. From personal and pastoral experience, I believe we need to reflect, review, rest—and pray for further wisdom—to ensure that the process has been authentic. Regrettably, it has to be said that some people will go to any lengths to *suggest* a reconciliation, but not *mean* it. The insincerity may be conscious or subconscious, but can prevent the restoration of harmony. It is vital, therefore, that we are 'as wise as serpents and as innocent as doves' in all this.

OUR WALK TO RECONCILIATION
In the Sermon on the Mount, Jesus taught us, *"Blessed are the pure in heart, for they will see God"* [Matthew 5:8]. To be pure in heart means, among other things, to will the things that God wants in

your life—more than anything else. The reward for those who do is indeed that they will see God.

In Genesis, there is a record of what happened the night before Jacob met Esau. He had already initiated their reconciliation, faced his fears, prayed his prayers and made his plans. He now had only to await his brother. That night, when Jacob was alone in his tent, God came to him. Jacob then had a most astonishing encounter with God. From that moment, he would walk through life in a new way. Nothing would ever be the same again. We are told that Jacob wrestled with God face to face, and God changed his name. He worked for peace and he saw God.

It would be all too easy to read the words in this chapter and yet do nothing about those relationships which we know need to be worked on. So why do something about them? We know there is no guarantee that they will turn out in the same way as for Jacob. We know that in our case there might be a need to go this way 'seventy times seven'. So why do it? The answer, surely, is in that prayer of Jesus for the unity of Christians; it is in the great command to love my neighbour; it is in that conditional clause in the Lord's prayer as we 'forgive those who sin against us'; and it is in the reward of obedience promised to the pure in heart in Matthew 5:8 '...for they will see God.'

For Jacob, that wonderful reconciliation—so costly and so hazardous—was one of the greatest moments of his life. Jacob humbled himself, and courageously did what was needed to heal the rift; then God came to him, and met with him in an amazing way. Surely all this should be motivation enough for us to begin to heal any ungodly divisions that we can and should repair.

PRAYER

*Heavenly Father, give me grace and courage
to engage in the act of reconciliation.
It is not easy; I naturally shy away from it—
but your word commands me to work through
difficult relationships, to the place of fellowship.
Father, give me success, I pray.*

Six

WRESTLING WITH GOD —THE TEST OF FAITH

Genesis 32:22–32

There was a time in Jacob's life when, having stepped out in faith, he found that his faith was put to the test. God had called Jacob to go home—to face his brother, claim his inheritance and play his part in the great purposes of God. As we have seen, Jacob obeyed God and headed home. In chapter five we saw how, on arriving in Canaan, he had first taken steps which would lead to the reconciliation with his brother. What we find in Genesis 32:22–32 is that God *tested* Jacob in this step of faith, before the reconciliation itself took place.

Let us look in greater depth at what Jacob went through at that point. We will see how relevant it is to us, as we go through similar times.

My explanation of these events is not the only one possible; there are several classic interpretations. It is sometimes taken to be an example of perseverance in prayer; or that we are being shown God breaking Jacob, and finally dealing with his sin of deception. I suggest, though, that what we see is Jacob being tested by God.

So what was it like for Jacob, as he went through this testing of his faith?

THE FEATURES OF THE TEST

Several years ago, I took my driving test. Although I thought I had done well, the examiner told me that I had failed. In retrospect, I could see that he was right. Although my three point turn had been excellent, my reversing around a corner perfect, my hill start inspirational, and my use of the mirror good, what had let me down had been my emergency stop.

Before my test, my instructor gave me a final session. He showed me where the emergency stop would, in all probability, take place, telling me that the examiner would call for the stop at a moment when the road behind was clear. So in the test, when we came to that road, I was ready!

As we set off, the examiner said that he would indicate the need to make an emergency stop by tapping the front window. I was focused and ready. As we drove down the road, I looked in my rear view mirror to see if there was anything behind us. There wasn't. Turning my eyes to re-focus on the road, from the corner of my eye I saw the examiner move. Instantly, I went for it, pressing hard down on the brake pedal. The car screeched to a stop, without stalling. An audience might have applauded.

So why did I fail on the emergency stop? The examiner's movement that I had seen was not to indicate the need to do an emergency stop but a raising of his hand to wipe his nose. To the man's complete surprise, I had brought the car to a sudden stop.

You may identify with my experience of taking a driving test and, maybe, my problems with the emergency stop. The reason for that is that there is a uniformity to the test. Most of us know what it is like to be tested in those various areas of driving skill.

It is extremely unlikely that you will ever go through exactly the same test as Jacob's, but we can all identify with it. The reason is that its characteristics are uniform with most, if not all, of God's testing of our faith.

So what were the features of Jacob's test of faith? In the first place, we are told that Jacob found himself in a wrestling match: *So Jacob was left alone, and a man wrestled with him...* [32:24]. As we can see from the passage, this was a bout which Jacob really did experience—not a merely metaphorical way of describing some sort of inward, psychological state of turmoil, nor just an intellectual struggle. An objective encounter actually occurred. For most people, however, their wrestling with God or testing of faith, would be figurative. It could be 'wrestling' that comes about because they find themselves ill, have fallen on hard times, as in the case of Job; or because they are asked to do a difficult thing, as when Philip was asked by Jesus where bread was to be bought to feed the five thousand who had gathered. (See John 6:5.) Sometimes the test comes because one is asked to make a great sacrifice, as with Abraham, or told to do an apparently foolish thing, as on the occasion when Gideon had to let many of his fighting men go home. Jacob's test was one where he really found himself grappling with an opponent.

The second thing we notice is that, initially, Jacob did not know that the identity of his opponent was the Lord: *Jacob said, "Please tell me your name"* [32:29]. When you first read this story, it is not immediately obvious who Jacob's opponent is. Visualise the scene in which Jacob is having to wrestle the other person whilst at the same time trying to discern the source of the attack. That initial uncertainty is an intended feature of the narrative. It is not until they have been fighting for some time that Jacob enquires as to the name of his opponent.

It is the same with us. Often, we go through a testing of our faith, whilst being unaware at first of who it is that we are fighting. Jacob found himself fighting God. Below the surface of our encounters, He is usually our 'opponent' too.

Neither was it obvious to Jacob that this was a test. The suggestion that he did not know the identity of his assailant carries with it the implication that he had no idea as to the purpose of this attack. A Christian caught up in such a conflict might at first be tempted to wonder whether this was an attack from the enemy; or, perhaps, from one with whom reconciliation has recently taken place; or as a consequence of past sin. (Did Jacob wonder, perhaps, whether Laban had caught up with him, intent on killing him?) Or is it just a result of living in the world? The times are evil: perhaps a mugger is attacking.... Can we identify with those thoughts? We so often miss out on what God is doing by making quick assumptions, which are so often inappropriate.

A further feature of Jacob's time wrestling is that it lasted for a specific duration—for one night, in his case ...*a man wrestled with him till daybreak* [32:24]. For us, it can be a shorter or a longer period. Abraham wrestled over the death of his son for several days; Joshua had seven days of wrestling with God's unique strategy for taking Jericho; Gideon had an extended period of time of wrestling with God over the loss of his men; Job was ill for months. The people of Israel were tested in the wilderness by God for forty years; Philip's test may have lasted for just a few moments.

Observe, too, that the longer Jacob fought, the more difficult things became:

When the man saw that he could not overpower him, he touched the socket of Jacob's hip so that his hip was wrenched as he wrestled... [32:25].

To have your faith tested, as you will know if you have undergone the experience, is not an easy thing. You may easily find yourself riddled with doubts. What is more, when the pressure is on, it is surprising how you can find yourself wrestling with your own shadows, such as poor self-image, past wrongs (probably long since repented of and forgiven), or even demonic chains of condemnation and guilt. The cure for the former, of course, is to stand upon the biblical promises and statements concerning your status as a child of the heavenly Father; and, as for those chains, to speak and declare the victory of Christ at Calvary over all the assaults of the enemy.

As Jacob wrestled, God decided to weaken His opponent, to make him less able to fight. Rather than getting easier, the battle became still worse. Because of the infirmity God inflicted on Jacob, he found himself having to fight harder and harder, just to maintain his position as he wrestled. As we consider the nature of God's testing, and its impact upon us, we do well to look at the effect of such tests upon other biblical characters. For Abraham, the test must have become much more intense during the period after he had been told to go and sacrifice his son, because God did not talk to him again until his boy was on the altar. For Job, after allowing him to become sick, He allowed some unhelpful friends to come on the scene. In the case of Gideon, after telling him to go and fight the Midianites, God then reduced his army. I have known God tell me to do something, and then He has not allowed the results of that action to follow on immediately. I have had to wait.

Next, notice how God used the right time to carry out the test— although Jacob himself would not have seen anything 'right' about

it. The passage shows us that, as well as making things worse for
Jacob the longer he fought, God had initiated the contest at what
would have seemed to Jacob a most inopportune time. Jacob was
already having to face some really difficult issues. His homecoming
after twenty years, was to face his brother whom he had cheated
and treated badly. What is more, it looked as if Esau was not coming
on the friendliest of terms: *Jacob looked up and there was Esau,
coming with his four hundred men...* [33:1].

When we look at the purpose of this test of faith, we will
understand why all this was happening, but first we should
appreciate the pressure Jacob was being put under. We are meant
to understand that God initiated all this. God had taken it upon
Himself, during what was already a difficult time for Jacob, to
surprise him one night with a mysterious intruder who, apparently,
sought to take his life.

See, also, how God determined who would be involved in the
test:

*That night Jacob got up and took his two wives, his two
maidservants and his eleven sons and crossed the ford of the Jabbok.
After he had sent them across the stream, he sent over all his
possessions. So Jacob was left alone...* [32:22–24a].

This was between God and Jacob, and no one else. Often it is a
'one on one' encounter —great loneliness there. Sometimes it is
an entire family that faces the test of faith; sometimes it is a church
congregation. Always, it is God who determines the characters
involved.

Several years ago, just as we were leaving Bible college, Sarah
and I felt the Lord call us to go and work in Scotland. Obediently,
we followed the Lord's leading and, through a series of events, we
were offered a job in a large Presbyterian church. But there was
one problem. There was no house with the job, and the salary
would not enable us either to buy a house or rent one of the very
few flats available in this desirable part of Edinburgh. On one of
my visits to the parish, while out walking one day, I came across a
beautiful house. It had a large garden, was in the centre of the
parish—and it was empty. As one idealistically does in one's
immaturity and keenness, I went up to the house, and there at the
front door claimed this house for Sarah and myself, in Jesus' name.
Then I went off to the minister, to tell him where my wife and I

were going to live. To cut a long story short, the house turned out to be one of twenty council houses in the area and, according to the minister, would never be made available to us. 'Knowing' better, we applied to the council to be given the house. We heard nothing. Shortly before the end of the college course, just a few weeks before we were to move, Sarah got a phone call from the council, saying that they could give us a house in the neighbouring area, but not that one. When I got home I telephoned them, saying we wanted that one.

We travelled to Scotland, not knowing whether we would be given that house. The people at the church said no; the council had said no. As you can imagine, we felt we were in one of these tests of faith. Yes, we could live in the manse with the minister while he was on holiday, but what then? It was not one of the easiest car journeys to make.

For us, the step of faith was moving up to Edinburgh in the belief that God would give us that house. Our test of faith was not seeing our prayer or action answered immediately; having the council say no; having those from the church tell us it would never happen; having to stay in a house that we knew would be ours only for a short time. Some features of our test were like those experienced by Jacob.

As for the house? A couple of days after we moved to Scotland, the council contacted us to say that they had changed their minds!

THE PURPOSE OF THE TEST

Many years ago, whilst at school, I went with fifteen of my class for a week at an outdoor pursuits centre near Bala, North Wales. I had a great week, except for one activity: orienteering.

Although we had spent a morning being instructed on how to use a compass and read a map, when it came to doing it I just did not have a clue. Sadly, my partner and I not only got lost on the course, but when we did (accidentally) get back to base, we found that the others had all been bused back to the centre without us.

Unhappily for me, the ordeal was not over. That night, back at the centre, I was invited to speak to the rest of the people on how to orienteer! Although I cannot remember what I actually said, had I known then what I know now, it would probably have been along these lines: "When it comes to orienteering, there is a world of difference between *saying* you know and actually putting that knowledge into practice. In addition, when you are doing the practical test, when the pressure comes on, don't dump the principles and go for the easiest way out." This illustrates why, having taught us the principles of orienteering, they had then sent us out to actually do it.

What the passage shows is that the same reasoning seems to have been at work in God's dealing with Jacob. Having spoken to Jacob, God now wanted to give Jacob the chance to put the principles into practice. Had Jacob really grasped what was going on? Did he really believe that God had appeared to him, and was calling him home to take up his inheritance and seek reconciliation with his brother? If he did believe, was Jacob—the previous deceiver who would often look for the easy way out—willing to stand his ground and walk by faith, even when it got difficult? There was only one way to find out. The pressure had to be applied. It was time for a practical test.

God wanted to see if He could overcome Jacob. When it comes to having your faith tested, it certainly feels as though you are in danger of being overcome. In Jacob's case, such pressure would come best from facing his greatest fear, the one that he had only recently prayed about, namely having to fight his brother. That night, as Jacob waited to meet with Esau, God, in the guise of a mysterious intruder, came to Jacob and engaged in a fight with him.

In order that what was truly in Jacob's heart would be revealed, God was opening him up. This is why having one's faith tested is such a painful thing: it is like coming under God's microscope. It tends to happen just as the temperature is being turned up, and all the germs in one's life are popping their heads up.

It has been said that our hearts are like gardens: somewhere we walk and commune with the Lord. Being tested opens them up to the scrutiny of an expert gardener. We are told that this was the purpose of the testing of the people of Israel: that God might see what was truly in their hearts. (See Deuteronomy 8:2.)

In my experience, this, more than anything else, is what helps you move into a truer understanding of what you truly believe of God; and, indeed, the true nature and extent of your commitment to Him. 'Getting out of the boat' is difficult, but 'walking on water' can be considerably harder, especially when you begin to see those waves and feel that wind.

This was the testing environment into which God was bringing Jacob; this is the area into which He brings us on occasions—all so that He, and we, might know the true state of our hearts.

THE OUTCOME OF THE TEST

One Friday morning at my Bible college, Ken Newton—a man with the gift of ministering in words of knowledge—came to chapel prayers. He called me to the front and gave me a word he felt he had from the Lord—to the effect that God, although delighted with my faith, wanted to refine it and make it stronger. Unbeknown to Ken, only the previous day, after watching a Reinhard Bonnke film about the evangelisation of the masses, I had asked God for faith that was as real as Reinhard's.

Ever since that day, my life has been extremely challenging. This however, does not surprise me—nor should it surprise you, if that is your Christian experience! 1 Peter 1:7 makes it clear that such challenges are God's way of accomplishing the maturing of our faith.

What was God seeking to accomplish in Jacob?—The same thing He seeks to accomplish in all of us: the maturing and refining of faith, and the establishing and praising of His name. Is that what He did in Jacob's life? The narrative suggests that it was. God found that He could not overcome Jacob: Jacob's faith was strong. God also found that Jacob had grown to the point where he would not let God go until He blessed him. So pleased with Jacob was God that He changed his name to testify to the fact that his faith was strong.

When it comes to walking by faith, and being tested in our faith, there is no guarantee that the end result will always be as good as it was for Jacob. Hebrews 11 shows us that there were many who walked by faith, and were tested in it, yet did not see their reward in this life. For everyone in a position like that of Joshua, who saw his Jericho fall down, there are others who did not see realised that which God had called them to believe for—that was their test of faith: believing but never seeing.

Whether or not we are aware of the fact, the eternal work which God was doing in Jacob will be ours, too. God tests us that He might refine and mature our faith. This was the outcome for Jacob, and God intends that a mature and refined faith will be ours, too. Again, we remember, He is seeking to do us good, not to destroy us.

But how exactly does God do what has to be done? How was God doing this refining and maturing? In applying the pressure to

Jacob, and consequently opening up his heart, God was then able to minister to him, and the text suggests several ways in which this process may have moved forward. The wrestling with God may have been for any of a number of reasons.

For example, it could have brought to the surface any weaknesses in his faith. As I have already intimated, Jacob was beginning to feel nervous about his forthcoming meeting with his brother. Only God knew what other difficulties Jacob might have to face. It was important that if there were any weak links in Jacob's faith they should be identified and sorted out now. Having this pressure applied could help Jacob identify where they were and give God the opportunity to address them.

Or, again, the test could have been to stimulate Jacob's faith. One of the ways you develop muscles is by exercising them. God knew that, in the near future, Jacob would have to rely on what He had said to him. A time would come when he would have to be strong. The wrestling with God was God's pre-ordained workout for Jacob; it was an opportunity for Jacob to 'work out' in God's presence the promises God had given him. To change the metaphor, God was working the soil so that the roots would go deeper.

Ultimately, the purpose of the test could have been to see Jacob's faith approved. God knew that Jacob believed, and was delighted by it. But, more than just being delighted, God also wanted to applaud Jacob for this step and act of faith. Consequently, in the dead of night God came to Jacob to honour him. It might look like it is Jacob who is calling the shots, but it is in fact God. We know that God wanted to change Jacob's name. This was the process through which God did that, and therefore through which He honoured him: *Then the man said, "Your name will no longer be Jacob, but Israel, because you have struggled with God and with men and have overcome"* [Genesis 32:28].

Although we cannot be certain of the ultimate purpose behind Jacob's experience of wrestling with God, we can be sure that it was a life enhancing moment. Ultimately, our tests will prove beneficial, as well.

WHY STAY IN THE FIRE?
Finally, let me offer something to encourage you to 'fight back' rather than run away, when God initiates a test in your life; to do the wrestling, instead of trying to evade it.

In America, there is a church which holds what it calls a Student Recognition Day, on the Sunday between Christmas Day and New Year's Day. On this occasion, the young people of the church who are students at colleges or universities, are asked to go up to the platform and give reports as to how their educational experiences have been going. It is a very important service for the older members of the church because many of them never had the educational opportunities that have been given to these young people, so they love to hear about all that has been happening to them.

On one such Sunday, after six of the young people had given their reports, the Pastor of the church stood up and gave some closing remarks.

"Children", he said, "you're going to die. You might not think you are, but you are. One of these days, they're going to take you out to the cemetery, drop you in a hole, throw some dirt on your face, and go back to church and eat potato salad. When you were born, you alone were crying and everyone else was happy. The important question I want to ask you tonight is: 'When you die are you going to be happy, leaving everyone else crying?' The answer depends on whether you have got titles or testimonies. When they lay you in the grave, are people going to stand around reciting the fancy titles you earned, or are they going to stand around giving testimonies of the good things that you have done for them and for God? Will it be degrees or blessings? Will it be newspaper obituaries or living letters? There is nothing wrong with titles; titles are a good thing to have. But when it comes down to it, go for the testimony."

Then the Pastor went on a poetic rip through the Bible as he mentioned those who had titles and those who had testimonies: Pharaoh may have had the title, but Moses had the testimony; Nebuchadnezzar may have had the title, but Daniel had the testimony; Jezebel may have had the title, but it was Elijah who had the testimony. Having brought the congregation to the climactic point, he finished with the most contrasting one of all: Pilate may have had the title, but Jesus had the testimony.

Why should we go through the testing times and seek to respond to them as well as we can, no matter what the cost? So that, just like Jacob, we might be numbered amongst those who have the testimony, and have been refined and matured by the living God, who loves us and with whom we shall dwell for eternity.

When you get to heaven, no-one is going to be interested in your titles; it will be your testimony that counts. Not only that, but even before then, when the going gets tough, it will be our testimonies that will keep us going.

As he wrestled with God, Jacob's life was totally changed. He didn't have the same name; he didn't walk in the same way, and he had discovered a new place: Peniel. What a testimony; what a story. Ours can be, too.

PRAYER

Heavenly Father, in times of testing,
help me to see what you are doing;
Help me to work with you, and to grow in my faith.
Father, I want to be one of your children with testimonies—
stories that bring glory to your name.
Lead me on in the great adventure of faith, I pray.

Seven

THE UPS AND DOWNS OF LIFE

Genesis 34–47

The story is told of a girl who went off to college and then did not write or contact her parents for a very long time. After a while, the girl began to feel really bad about this, so she wrote them this letter:

Dear Mummy and Daddy,

I am sorry that since leaving for university I have not been very good about keeping in touch with you. I will bring you up to date, but before you read on, please sit down. I am pleased to say that I am progressing quite well, now that the skull fracture I sustained when I jumped out of my hall of residence window (when there was a fire shortly after my arrival) is getting better. It has just about healed. I now only get migraines once a day. Fortunately, the fire in my building, and the jump, was witnessed by a cleaner at the nearby petrol station. He took me to hospital, where he stayed with me. On my discharge from hospital, I was homeless because of the burnt out condition of the college rooms, so he kindly asked me to share his basement bedsitter with him. It is very tiny but rather sweet. He is a fine boy and we have fallen deeply in love and plan to marry. Although we have not set the exact date yet, we think it will be before my pregnancy begins to show.

Yes, Mum and Dad, I am pregnant! I know how joyfully you will anticipate being grandparents and that you will warmly welcome the baby, giving it the same love and care you have given me. The reason we have not fixed a date for our wedding is my boyfriend's infection (which I carelessly caught from him.) I am confident you will welcome him into our family. He is kind and, though uneducated, does have ambition. While he belongs to an ethnic minority and a different religion, I know that your tolerance (which you have so often spoken about) will prevent you from fretting about all that.

Having caught up with the 'news' Mum and Dad, I now want to tell you the truth. There was no fire, I did not have a fractured skull, nor was I in hospital. I am pleased to say that I am neither pregnant nor infected—there is not even a boyfriend. However, I did fail one exam this term, so will have to resit it, and I really hope what I have written above will help you to see this in its true perspective and keep it in proportion!

How vital it is to have a proper perspective on things! Any caring parent who has been through the trials and tribulations which so often attend young people's exams will understand exactly why the girl might have written as she did. It is so often hard to keep things in proportion....

In Genesis 34–47, we are given a 'warts and all' account of a man who attempted to walk with God. That would be a fair description of the way most Old Testament characters are depicted. One of the reasons why the Bible gives us such a full and frank life story of Jacob is so that we may have a proper perspective on what it means to be a follower of God.

My purpose in this chapter is to examine what it means to be a follower of God. What can we expect to experience in our lives? What effect will the passage of life's events have upon us? How should we respond to our daily lot—and what is God's place in all of this?

In his book entitled *Carpe Diem*, Tony Campolo tells of a question he once posed to his class of academics. Although not academically challenging, the question proved difficult for them to answer. As Campolo explained, the difficulty was not that it made them think hard but that it made them think honestly.

Campolo's question was this: "How long have you truly lived?". The question clearly did not mean: "How long have you existed on this planet?" Most of them would have answered that with: "twenty four years or so". It meant, rather, "How much of your life have you truly grasped the moment and lived in the reality and significance of it? How long have you *truly* lived?" Campolo reckons that most people go through life without really living.

When Jacob met God at Bethel, one of the things that came out of that encounter was an ability to truly live; to live in a heightened awareness of each and every moment. That is God's gift to all believers. What the writer of the Genesis passages gives us, as he takes us 'through the keyhole' into Jacob's life, is a description of all the places and landmarks, all the valleys and mountains, within which Jacob truly lived, and that includes scenarios that we can identify with in our lives.

In Ecclesiastes chapter nine, Solomon concludes his search for a life worth living, setting out his understanding of the realities of life; helping us to see what is left after you have stripped out the myths and the 'maybes'.

Solomon identified four major realities of life, and they are headings within which the main characteristics of Jacob's life can be grouped.

The first major feature was the continual proximity of death. We are told that during his life, Jacob saw his wife Rachel die in childbirth (35:16); his father die (35:27–29); his grandson die; and he had reason to believe that his son, Joseph, had died. He encountered natural death (father), tragic death (wife), premature death (grandson), and what appeared to be death in suspicious circumstances (Joseph).

Secondly, there was for Jacob the nearness of evil and insanity. Solomon teaches that within the heart there is evil and madness; as well as maybe having such things within our own hearts, we can also become victims of these forces as we suffer the results of others' insanity. This was the case in Jacob's life. Although we are not made aware of Jacob actually acting insanely during this period, we are told that he was the victim of such actions on the part of others. His daughter, Dinah, was raped by one of the local boys (Genesis 34). Two of his sons deceived the villagers where Dinah's rapist lived, killing them all. Because of jealousy over Joseph, his boys sold him as a slave to be sold in Egypt. Reuben, the eldest, slept with Jacob's concubine (35:22).

Thirdly, Jacob's life was marred by uncertainty. Solomon told us that:

...The race is not to the swift, or the battle to the strong,
nor does food come to the wise or wealth to the brilliant

or favour to the learned;
but time and chance happen to them all.
[Ecclesiastes 9:11].

In Genesis 42–47, we learn that the whole world was engulfed in a massive famine. Jacob lived through each day not knowing if it would be his last. There was uncertainty hanging over the life of his family, and over whether or not they could feed their animals. Moreover, in the events that surrounded his sons' journey to Egypt to buy food, there was the further uncertainty as to whether he would see his son Simeon again, and then whether or not he would see his son Benjamin again. When it was discovered that Joseph was alive, and inviting him to Egypt, there was the initial uncertainty as to whether this was a right move or not.

The final major feature of Jacob's life was that he experienced some hope. Life for Jacob was not all doom and gloom. Jacob would have agreed with Solomon's saying that *even a live dog is better off than a dead lion!* Among the hopeful events was the birth of Benjamin, a second son from the womb of his beloved wife Rachel (and some consolation, following the loss of Joseph). In the midst of the famine, there was the news of food in Egypt; then the discovery that Joseph was alive; his meeting with God at Bethel, where the covenant was re-affirmed, and the changing of his name acknowledged; the opportunity to talk to, and bless, Pharaoh.

What is the application of all this for those of us who are followers of God today? We are reminded, in the first place, that many of the things a person of faith experiences in life will be similar to what everyone else has to cope with. We may be 'saints' (in the proper, biblical sense), but we are not thereby insulated from reality. We have to cope with bereavement, loneliness, unemployment, sickness and family difficulties, just as unbelievers have to.

It is true that, at times, God delivers us from some of these things—but this is not often the case. The God of the Bible is not a God who removes us from the realities of life. Our life, as followers of God, could best be described as being on an assault course, on which many unexpected difficulties and surprising events are to be found. That was a picture a friend had for me when I was going through a difficult time, and I have seen it as an accurate account of many of life's difficult events ever since. It was Jacob's lot, and

Solomon saw it as man's lot in a more universal way.

How often we are tempted to think, 'if only...', and to dwell on how much better, more enjoyable, more fulfilling, and less problematic others' lives are. That is, of course, a colossal illusion. Other people's problems are every bit as bad as yours! Instead of such fruitless envy of the lot of someone else, thank God that, in the midst of all your trials, you have Him.

Secondly, there is the matter of our witness. The Scripture teaches us that we are to be ready to give a reason for the hope that is within us, and makes it clear that, as a church, our God-given mandate is to bring the gospel to the world. Our witness, of course, includes what we experience of the love and power of God in the real contexts of life. Effective witnessing takes seriously, and addresses, all the realities of life—its uncertainties, the evil we encounter, and the madness of which the world has produced so much; as well as then focusing our hearers on the hope which is offered to mankind only by the God and Father of our Lord Jesus Christ.

As we obey the biblical command to go out and make disciples, it is vital that, as we go, we understand the message that we have to take, and how it relates to those around us. We should be recognizable as those who have embraced life and its realities, not withdrawn from it. Whilst we might not be able to answer all the questions about life, we do have some real answers, and we must not be ashamed of them. Jesus Christ is the true answer to the real problems of living, for he alone is the Way, the Truth and the Life. Christians have all too often failed to understand the nature of society and lacked the boldness to apply biblical truths to our engagement with it.

The life of Jacob shows us what the realities of life are and, in relationship with Jesus, we can face up to them, ready for the 'assault course', equipped with the Word of God and the resources of the Holy Spirit.

THE EFFECT OF LIVING TODAY

When we took our children to Euro Disney, we had an absolutely fantastic time. The children loved the rides, the shows, and all the characters, and they were in their element. For me, the best ride of all was the *Star Wars* simulator. The intention is to give you an experience which is as close as possible to what it would have been like to fly in the 'Star Wars' film. Through the movement of the Shuttle, the use of music, and visual effects displayed on the screen, we felt the drama and danger, fear and excitement, dread and anticipation. When I left the capsule, I honestly felt that I had ridden amongst the stars! I felt exhausted, having entered fully into what was on screen, living every moment. It took me a little while after the ride to calm down. It was one of the best funfair rides of my life.

But in comparison with the ride that life itself gives us, the 'Star Wars' ride, or any other simulation, no matter how exciting, pales into complete insignificance. We do well to remember this when we find we are becoming over-dependent on the stimulus of any form of 'entertainment', whether 'soaps', spectator sport or other kinds of diversion. There is so much that tends to anaesthetise us against the realities of life.

Our look at the life of Jacob has provided abundant confirmation of the primacy of actual experience. We have seen that Jacob's life was an astonishing ride through tough realities, amazing ups and downs, and that God used it all to build him up, refine him, mature him, and cause him to enter into a deeper relationship with Himself.

Consider again the effects of life's unexpected difficulties and events upon Jacob. He experienced a huge range of emotions.

Jacob knew what it meant...

...to wish that he were dead [37:34]
Although he does not use that form of words, he comes close to it. Just after Jacob had been told that his special son, Joseph, was dead, he came to a place where he wished his own life was over. He experiences a sense of meaninglessness:

Then Jacob tore his clothes, put on sackcloth and mourned for his son many days. All his sons and daughters came to comfort him, but he refused to be comforted. "No," he said, "in mourning will I go down to the grave to my son." So his father wept for him.

... to be 'stunned' [45:25–26]
On the second return of his sons from Egypt, they brought news to Jacob that Joseph was not dead after all; and that, in fact, he was now the second most powerful man in Egypt. On hearing this, Jacob was stunned and speechless. He entered that zone where there are no emotions, just numbness. We learn that so

overcome with numbness was Jacob that he found himself unable to believe what his sons had to say to him:

So they went up out of Egypt and came to their father Jacob in the land of Canaan. They told him, "Joseph is still alive! In fact, he is ruler of all Egypt." Jacob was stunned; he did not believe them.

...to be fearful [34:30]
After Jacob's daughter, Dinah, had been raped, two of Jacob's sons, unbeknown to him, attacked the rapist's home village, killing all the menfolk. Jacob naturally feared that this could provoke the neighbouring clans to attack them. He was overcome with fear.

Then Jacob said to Simeon and Levi, "You have brought trouble on me by making me a stench to the Canaanites and Perizzites, the people living in this land. We are few in number, and if they join forces against me and attack me, I and my household will be destroyed."

...to be broken [35:16–20]
In the midst of what should have been a very proud and joyous moment for Jacob—the birth of his second child by Rachel—the moment was turned into a nightmare, as his wife so suffered during the birth that she died just moments afterwards. Although Jacob's reaction is not described, we can well imagine how devastating it must have been.

...to be 'revived' [45:27]
Jacob knew what it meant to be given a new lease of life; to enter the springtime of life after being in what had seemed an eternal winter. What was it that brought this glorious morning bursting into his life? It was the news that Joseph was alive. Following his initial reaction of being stunned, after his sons had spoken further to him he became convinced by what he heard. It was like a new day dawning—more than he could ever have hoped for.

But when they told him everything Joseph had said to them, and when he saw the carts Joseph had sent to carry him back, the spirit of their father Jacob revived. And Israel said, "I'm convinced...."

...to be full of self pity [42:36]
To be at that point where you are so emotionally overwhelmed that you cannot think properly, and you feel that the whole world is against you—that life is against you. Here you have no friends,

and believe that everyone is your enemy.

Their father Jacob said to them, "You have deprived me of my children. Joseph is no more and Simeon is no more, and now you want to take Benjamin. Everything is against me!"

Reviewing the emotions Jacob experienced, we can only be moved by the way they parallel so much of our natural, human experience. It all has such a contemporary 'feel' to it, and we are reminded of the continuing applicability of the Bible to our situation. In no way is it 'old-fashioned'. We are dealing with eternal truths about what it is to be a human being.

GROWING IN GOD
As Jacob experienced this 'roller coaster' life, there grew in him a greater awareness of the presence and power of God.

In John's Gospel, we read of a marvellous moment, when the disciples are asked by Jesus where their loyalty lies. He has just given a magnificent talk about how, one day, people would 'eat his body' and 'drink his blood'. As a result, many of those who had followed him up to this point decided that this 'Jesus thing' was not a good idea after all, and left him. What Jesus wants to know is whether the disciples will do likewise. Peter answers: *"Lord, to whom shall we go? You have the words of eternal life"* [John 6:68], meaning: 'There is nothing out there for us; you are the answer; we must stay with you.'

So with Jacob: despite all that life had thrown at him, instead of being driven away from God, he was actually brought closer. These were some of the results:

Jacob learnt to really seek God [See 43:14 & 46:1]
Note that, as his boys are about to set out for Egypt a second time, Jacob's contribution to their trip is not only wisdom but also spirituality. He blesses them as they depart, praying that God will give them success. When he went to Egypt himself, he stopped on the way and enquired of God.

Jacob learnt obedience to the ways of God
God asks Jacob to go to Bethel, to meet with Him. He did. We are later told that Jacob came to his father's house—something he had earlier been commanded to do. Subsequently, the narrative

tells us that God told Jacob to go and stay in Egypt. Again, we learn that he followed God's command.

Jacob grew in the worship of God

He learnt to really worship God. We think of Bethel, and of his worship on the way to Egypt.

His life became marked by purity [35:2]

Following the rape of Dinah, God called Jacob to return again to Bethel. In obedience, Jacob responds. However, as he goes to Bethel, now really aware of the God that he is coming to meet with, he encourages all the people in his party to put away all foreign gods. They are going to worship the one true God. There is no place for false deities.

So Jacob said to his household and to all who were with him, "Get rid of the foreign gods you have with you, and purify yourselves and change your clothes."

He began to witness for God [35:3]

As well as sensing the need to get the people and his party right for his encounter with God at Bethel, he also took the opportunity to speak to them about the God that they were going to worship. To use evangelistic language, he gives them his testimony, telling them how this is the God who met with him all those years ago, and who has kept him safe.

Then come, let us go up to Bethel, where I will build an altar to God, who answered me in the day of my distress and who has been with me wherever I have gone.

He began to see God's view of the family

As Jacob passed through the troubles of life, he also experienced a heightened awareness of the importance of his family, especially the children God had given him.

We, too, need to grow in maturity, to the point where we have a right view of these things. How damaged our society is because we fail to prioritise our marriage partners and children, putting other things first instead.

We may speculate as to the role played in Joseph's growing openness to the things of the Spirit by his father's commitment to leading the boy in devotions, and helping him to appreciate the place of God in the family, during his childhood.

The Hebrew faith in God was taught and practised primarily in the setting of the family. How important it is, in our families, to build a foundation of worship; to help our children to know the reality of God.

Sadly, because of his love for Rachel, Jacob was unduly biased in favour of the two sons of Joseph and, later, Benjamin. But the brothers had matured sufficiently not to resent the latter during his time in Egypt, as they had done in the case of Joseph.

We know how the effects of living have the potential to wear us down. We have also seen enough of Jacob's journey through life's troubles to detect a syndrome which can pervade our lives, too. It is characterised by emotional turbulence; episodes of sin which have to be dealt with; and the exercise of a will which is not yet conformed to God's will. Jacob's emotional life, like ours, can go haywire. When we experience all this, it can be overwhelming, even to the point where you feel as if you would rather be dead.

One of the guys I play tennis with told me recently of a person at work who, five years after the death of his wife, still cannot get a handle on life. So bad is his condition that the company is in the process of making him unemployed.

Jacob's life shows us that such inner devastation should come as no surprise. We are shown that life's troubles can bring you to a point where you are out of your depth. But such times, if used rightly, can also have a positive effect. They can drive us to God and lead us to re-evaluate our priorities in a way which is truly healthy.

The problem is that our natural state is one of rebellion against God, and an illusion of self-sufficiency. Sooner or later, the troubles of life demonstrate to us the insupportable character of our natural state, and the incoherence of a view of life based upon it. We start to discover that there really is a great choice to be made in life. The option of obedience, and receiving from God what only He can provide, begins to appear in its true light as the right course. We begin to search; and we are promised that those who seek God will find Him.

When we make that life commitment, and come into contact with other Christians, we discover both the value of life in the body of Christ—and the imperfection of every local fellowship. There are so many ways in which the life of any local church falls short of God's best, but if there is at the heart of it a real grounding in the Scriptures and a desire to grow in obedience and faithfulness to Jesus Christ, then being with other Christians can help to nurture us on our own journey through life's troubles and joys; giving us the opportunity to deepen our own discipleship, and providing plenty of scope for sanctification as we exercise forgiveness and begin to appreciate others, and the reality of their journeys, too.

In every aspect of our corporate Christian life—worship times, pastoral groups or congregational life as a whole—there must be realism. We have to face the truth that we see so powerfully depicted in the life of Jacob: there are real troubles to be faced (in our own lives, and others' lives); there are battles to be fought and won; there can be real anguish and emotional distress. Such features of life are so easy to brush under the carpet and ignore. There must be no empty triumphalism; joy must be genuinely from the Spirit, not something we work up in ourselves; our praise and thanksgiving often has to be a decision or act of the will, rather than a reflection of how we feel, and God honours that. In all things, there is to be realism, not escapism. We are called to be people of integrity who help others face the issues and the often hurtful effects of life, in an atmosphere of truth, love and forgiveness. When you are going through the mill, it is great to have people to whom you can turn, who will listen, who will cry with you, and who will help if they can—folk who will be there for you. These things are among the blessings our churches need to be providing. The quality of unselfish, loving, caring Christian fellowship in the early church (though, even then, far from perfect) was profoundly attractive to many in a pagan society, and should be part of its attractiveness today, too.

Several years ago, when I lived in Swansea, some friends and I organised open air evangelistic events on the first Saturday of every month. It was interesting, sometimes, to observe the reactions of people as they passed the person giving out tracts. I once saw a middle aged man screw up the leaflet he had been given, then throw it on the ground. Always keen for a conversation, I picked up the paper, went after him and gave it back to him, saying he had dropped it, and asking why he had thrown it down. The man's response, after the shock and anger had surfaced, was to ask a question. How could he believe in a God of love after his father had died such a tragic death? Where was God when his father and mother needed Him most? Where was God when he had cried out for Him to come and help them? It was a good question. Where *was* God? It is a question Jacob could often have asked, as he passed through the unexpected troubles of life. Where was God in it all? We are given some answers to that question.

GOD WAS WITH JACOB THROUGH IT ALL

On the two occasions that God met with Jacob at Bethel, we learn that, through all he was to undergo, through each stage of the journey, He would be *with* him. God would be *for* him, and He would be *working out His purposes*.

In Jacob's fear, which stemmed from his sons' bad actions, God had promised to be with him. In Jacob's devastation, which came from thinking that his son Joseph was dead, God promised to be with him. In his having to deal with the people of Egypt to gain food, God would be for him. In the journey to Egypt, God indicated that He would be working out His purposes through him.

God was the God of Bethel. He was the God who had initiated their relationship, promising that, at each stage of the way, He would *be* there. Although the occasions when we see God move dramatically in Jacob's life may be few in number, we are shown that he was constantly given the opportunity to know the closeness of God.

Although God had promised to be with him, and, objectively, that was the spiritual reality, it is also true to say that at times Jacob *felt* that God was silent. At times, the *promise* was all that Jacob had to go on. This is a feature of the life of faith in every age: sometimes there are no feelings and no outward manifestations to show that God is with us.

That this is so is another aspect of the testing of our faith. Sometimes Jacob may well have felt that he was all alone. He may even have doubted that there was a God, let alone that God had led him and was for him; though that would have been less likely in those times, when theism of one sort or another was an integral part of the world view of most people—part of what we might term the 'mental furniture' which went with the cosmology of that age.

Occasionally, God intentionally removed Himself from Jacob's consciousness, in order to draw him on. Sometimes the events of life blanked out any sense of God's presence. So in the midst of having God's presence in reality, there were times when he felt that heaven was silent—an experience with which we can all identify, or which we can, at least, understand. At such times, the *footprints in the sand* story is probably the true state of affairs. As we look back, we will see only one set of footprints—evidence of the Lord carrying us. The cry that comes from a sense of abandonment is one that rages through the Bible. It was often the cry of the psalmist; it was the cry of Elijah; it was the cry at Golgotha, and it has been the cry of many a saint in the history of Christendom.

At times when it is our cry, what we must do is not rely on our feelings but hold true to the Scriptures; the commands and promises of the precious, revealed Word of God. Faith is to be distinguished from both feelings and intellectual knowledge.

GOD AFFIRMED JACOB'S ACTIONS [46:1–4]
One of the toughest and most crucial moments in Jacob's life came when he had the invitation to go into Egypt and live with his son Joseph. The promise of God was that Jacob would inherit the land in which he was now resident. This was the promise that had come to his grandfather and to his father, and had now come to him. But there was now a famine and they could not survive in this land. They could go to Egypt; there they would have food, shelter and a good life.

But what about the promise? God had not said anything about the time in Egypt. Should Jacob stay with the promise? Should he read the circumstances as guidance from God? Was moving to Egypt sinful, as it was for his grandfather, Abraham, or was it God's way out of this very difficult and potentially devastating famine?

As sometimes happens when one seems to need guidance most, God was then silent, making Jacob sweat and think it through. Only *after* Jacob had made his move did God step in and assure him that it was the right one.

LIVING WITH GOD AND TROUBLE
We have thought about the significance of many of these things for our own lives. As it was for Jacob, so it often is for us.

God was with Jacob: He is with us, too, whether or not we are subjectively aware of that fact. Scripture makes it clear that He is with us, He is for us, and He will work out everything in accordance with His promises. This assurance may not solve all the mysteries of life, but what an encouragement to us as we go through both the good and the troubled times.

Just as it sometimes seemed to Jacob that God was distant, so it may be for us. In the Song of Songs, there is a time when the lover removes himself from the bride and goes out into the night. In desperation, the bride goes in search of her lover. Anxious to find him, she looks everywhere, but he cannot be found. Such times of loneliness and the feeling of being deserted is 'par for the course' in the Christian life.

Whether to develop our maturity, to test us, or because good will result in the end, there will be times when we are allowed to experience moments when we feel alone. Sometimes, it seems, God will leave us to make a decision ourselves, and then, later, confirm it. Again, to develop us and to mature us, as we go on in the Christian walk, God sets greater and greater tests before us, to humble us—not as a punishment for sin, but rather that He might help us grow in our faith.

It is a tremendous blessing and encouragement to us to read of Jacob's Bethel—that very special place in his life. It is also valuable for us to keep a record of *our* 'Bethels'—the times when *we* encounter God, in whatever way. For the rest of his life, Jacob remembered what had happened there, the promises which were given, and the significance of it all. Memories of what God has said and done are significant, but our ability to remember details does vary and, often, the power of recollection diminishes with the passage of time. I keep a journal, and commend the practice to you as being a helpful one. Have a book in which you record all the things that God says to you and does for you. Note down, as well, the scriptures that seem to 'come alive' with special significance. It will become, for you, an aid to navigating through your life, something to keep next to your Bible. It will give you refreshment at those times when it seems that God has withdrawn Himself from you. With such a record, it is possible to return to your own personal Bethel, again and again, without leaving your armchair. My journal helps me recall and testify accurately to the ways in which God has led me. I can remember the ways in which He has provided a house, finance, and an engagement ring for Sarah. As I re-read what I recorded, I am reminded of the times when I have received words and pictures from Him, and occasions when He has used me. All this brings encouragement and refreshment of faith for one more day. But always remember that we cannot live only on our past experience of the Lord! As we move forward in our walk with Jesus, we look to him to go on speaking and guiding every day. A journal will not just point us back to those special moments, it always serves to remind us that our God speaks, guides, and reveals Himself to us in ways that are relevant for here and now.

In this chapter, we have looked a little more deeply at 'ups and downs' in the life of Jacob. Again, we have been reminded that the life of faith is not easy! In these 'me-centred' days, it can be a tough thing to take on board. The seed of the Word that is sown in your life needs to be nourished and watered; it is meant by God to put down deep roots. It takes spiritual nourishment, the constant in-filling of the Holy Spirit, and growing knowledge of the written word of God, for us to be properly equipped to deal with the tough and strenuous tasks which come with the way of faith.

As we observed in Chapter one, when we considered the distorted and unsatisfactory relationships in his family, Jacob's lot was very much like that of many other people who have to deal with such issues. It might seem, on the face of it, that his determination to follow God made things harder. This is one reason why some react against Christianity: there is a cross to bear, a narrow way to keep to, and a yoke to bear. But the truth is that the world's options are much worse. The cross of Jesus is the only way to peace and eternal life; the narrow way is for our good and his honour; the yoke is much easier than slavery to sin. The life of faith may be tough, but the alternative of fear and doubt leads to the place of destruction.

If you have responded to the call of Jesus Christ; handed over your life to him; invited him to be your only Lord and Saviour, then you are on the road of faith. Be assured that the toughness of the road will not harm you; through all of it God will be for you, and for your eternal good. Jesus said: *...no one can snatch them out of my hand* [John10:28]. If ever you are tempted to doubt the truth of this, look again at the promises of the risen Lord Jesus, recorded in the Book of Revelation. There are many, and they are intended to build us up and keep us faithful. Jesus tells us to: *'Be faithful, even to the point of death, and I will give you the crown of life'* [Revelation 2:10b].

If you are a mature Christian, you have a valuable part to play in the lives of others. You have a rich reservoir of experience and testimonies to share with the church. There are young families and individuals who are struggling with their walk with God. They are just discovering that life, including the life of faith, is tough.

You have something precious. Take the opportunities afforded you to give, sensitively, to others.

If you are struggling with life at this time, be comforted with the assurance which God gave to Jacob, that He was with him. He wants you to know the same assurance. We are not alone, but have with us, every step of the way, a loving, heavenly Father.

Let us heed the challenges of Jacob's life, seizing the day; really and truly living—in each moment that life affords us. It is so easy to waste time, but our time here on earth is limited. Opportunities never recur in the same way. So invite God to move fully into every area of your being: for good, and for eternity. God longs to give you the opportunity to glorify His name and to enjoy the abundant life that He has promised to all who love His Son, Jesus.

It has been said that our lives are like a tapestry being prepared by the Father. True, we cannot see the finished article yet. True, at times it looks as if there is nothing but endless pieces of yarn hanging all over the place. What we see now, as we reflect on our lives to date, is an unfinished story. But one day, God will finish the tapestry, and for all eternity it will be in the courts of heaven as a testimony to His faithfulness and grace. Like many metaphors, this tells only part of the story. The truth it conveys is that, amid the troubles and joys of life, God is working His purpose out. To use a biblical picture: He is the potter; we are the clay, and we do well to remember that truth in an age when we are sold the illusion that we are in charge.

But the tapestry image does not tell the whole truth, for, amazingly, we shall be transformed, and our final appearance, in heaven, will lack the defects and sins and sadnesses, the tears and shortcomings, which the tapestry might display today. ...*We will be changed* [1 Corinthians 15:52]. When we received Jesus Christ, we were washed clean by his blood; when we meet the Father He will look upon us and see the glory of Jesus, for we are in him and he dwells in us. Our garments will be wholly pure. There won't be any messy, sinful, unhealed or unholy bits in us when we are in heaven.

Jacob had to come to a place of real, personal trust in God—the same God who draws us to Himself, sanctifies us, and gives us new life 'in Christ' as we respond to His Word. We, too, need to trust Him, no matter what the circumstances or troubles we may have to pass through.

PRAYER

Heavenly Father, thank you for my life.
Help me to include you in every aspect of it, every day.
When times are tough, give me awareness of your presence.
When times are good, give me a heart of thankfulness.
Father, today I commit my life and this day, afresh, to you.
Do within it that which you desire to do.

Eight

DYING WELL

Genesis 47:28–50:17

Some funerals are much harder to conduct than others. I recall one which was especially problematic. The deceased had evidently been greatly disliked by many folk, because of his eccentricities. Relationships with others had been exceptionally strained. Much tougher than this, from my point of view, was that he seemed to have been an unbeliever. That makes it an uphill task for the minister to find appropriate things to say in the address. What a joy it can be, in contrast, to share in the funeral of a believer, whose life has reflected something of the goodness of God, and whose legacy is of positive relationships and hope in the family.

Jacob's death, and the response of his family to it, was of the latter kind. The passage to which we now turn is rather like an invitation to join Jacob in the last few days of his life, and then to observe his family around the time of the funeral. The text makes it abundantly clear that Jacob's faith in God's promises and blessings was alive right up to the point of his death. He took joy and delight in his family, and they loved and respected him. What an inspiration that is for us.

The reason for the title of this chapter is, of course, the way Jacob died. His death had a quality that I would be happy to experience myself; I suggest that all of us would, when the time comes. As Jacob prepared for his death, we find a man who was filled with hope, surrounded by peace, and with an overwhelming consciousness of the presence of God.

So, as we conclude this study, let us look at the great issue of how one may die well.

When we consider Jacob's life as a whole, there are many lessons we can apply to our own lives. But the death of Jacob is undoubtedly of the greatest relevance to all of us—for we all die.

We may not be as aware of the imminence of death as Jacob was. We might not be granted as long to prepare for it as he was. We might have more pain. We do not know when we shall die; that is in the hands of God. But it is possible to die well, like Jacob.

The death that Jacob died was, in many senses, prepared for decades beforehand. Only some of the arrangements were last minute ones. It can be the same for us.

So how does a follower of God die well? Let us look at how Jacob died, and why we can say that his death was such a good one.

DEATH WITH FAITH [Genesis 47:28–31]
One of the most moving funerals I have attended was that of a four year old. Despite the tragic nature of the boy's death, there can be no disputing that the funeral was filled with hope and faith, particularly on the part of the parents.

I am the resurrection and the life, were the words that the vicar read out, as he led the coffin into the crematorium. The resurrection was, without doubt, the overriding feature of the service. This young lad had known he was dying, and he knew where he was going. His family knew he was dying and where he was going. Consequently, they knew that one day, some day, they would see him again. This was not the end, only a momentary goodbye.

Of all that Jacob went through in this life, and, as we have seen, he went through an awful lot, what the Bible celebrates in a most remarkable way is the *attitude* with which he died. Jacob is honoured for his faith in God for the future; his death is such a hopeful one.

This final episode of the Jacob narrative begins as he summons Joseph to his side. He is about to die but, before he does, it is important for him that the arrangements be made as to the site of his grave. He wants to be buried in the homeland, with his father and his grandfather. So important to Jacob is the site of his burial that he gets Joseph to swear under his thigh that he will carry out that which he has requested. With Joseph's agreement, Jacob leaned on his staff, and he worshipped God. This leaning on the staff, which Hebrews 11:21 commends him for, holds a key place in the narrative. His staff is not only his walking stick, it represents Jacob's pilgrimage—his journey through life, with God.

Jacob believes that, one day, God will fulfil His promise to him and give to his descendants the land of Canaan. He does not know *when* God will fulfil His word, but he knows by faith in God's word that it *will* be so. He has faith in God for the future, so he requests that he be buried back in Canaan, the land of promise. He wants to be where the future of his descendants will lie.

I think we would be right to suggest that, as well as believing God for His promise that his descendants will inherit the land, Jacob also has faith in God as to his personal future in the afterlife. We are not told of any formal view on this question. Nowhere are we told that these early Hebrews had a developed view of resurrection. But there is a belief in God being the God of the living. In some undeveloped way, Jacob sees that there is hope for him beyond the grave. Hence his wanting to be gathered with his ancestors.

A friend of mine, who works with the terminally ill, tells me that she often finds a real faith and hope in Christians who are about to die. There is a stark contrast with the atheist, who faces (he or she believes) non-existence. Jacob's attitude, as he faced death, communicates a profound confidence in the eternal purposes of God; he displays such assurance that we can scarcely conceive that he could contemplate anything but a future existence with the God whose faithfulness he trusted absolutely. Jacob believed that his future was safe with God. Everything he is recorded as having said and done in those final encounters with the family speaks volumes about his faith, even in the absence of explicit evidence concerning a view of resurrection.

Such a sure confidence in God's eternal purpose for us (and for our descendants, too) should mark our hope and our faith. We can trust God in regard to our eternal resting place—not merely because, intellectually, it makes more sense to believe in life after death (though it does), but because of the promises of Jesus himself to believers, and because of the promises of God in the rest of the New Testament. These are not merely the plausible ideas of men; they are God's revealed truth.

As to what we shall leave behind us: where we have worked within and according to the purposes of God, we can be confident that, although we might not see the promise which accompanied our particular calling fulfilled in our own lifetime, nonetheless one day it will be fulfilled.

WITH THANKFULNESS [Genesis 48:15-16]

At Bible college, every student preached a 'leaving sermon' after which the Principal prayed personally for the leaver. I vividly remember his prayer for me; it was more than a prayer, becoming more akin to a word of prophecy. He thanked God that, at the end of my life, I would be able to look back and see how He had so marvellously led me.

As he looked back over his days, Jacob could be thankful for the leading of God in his life. God had been his shepherd, leading him back from Laban to Canaan; taking him to Bethel; leading him into Egypt.

But far more than just being his leader, God had also been a provider for him—another aspect of shepherding. God had fed Jacob. We recall, especially, Joseph's presence in Egypt during the famine.

Even more than this, God had been Jacob's protector. In his prayer of thanks, Jacob can talk of the angel who has delivered him from all harm. We recall those occasions in Jacob's life when he encountered an angel: when Laban came to hurt him; when he started his journey back to Canaan and he came to two camps, and saw the fighting angel of God; and there had been that remarkable time of 'wrestling'.

In all these things, he saw, and was thankful for, God's hand upon his life. However, the truly marvellous thing about Jacob is that it was not just during his last days that he became thankful to God. We can see Jacob's heart of thankfulness toward God expressed throughout his life in the way that he built many altars of worship—altars which were sometimes physical, sometimes confessional. He built one at Bethel, when God met with him whilst he was running away from home. He built one as he talked with his wives, as he planned to leave Paddam Aram. He built one after his peace treaty with Laban. He built one at Mahanaim, when he saw the angels of God. He built one at Peniel, after he had fought with God. He built one in the midst of his family, as he went to Bethel again. He built another on his third visit to Bethel, and another at Beersheba, as he and his family headed for Egypt.

As his death draws near, we find that he builds another one. There, in front of his son Joseph, in the company of his two grandsons, Jacob takes a few moments to thank the God who has been the shepherd of his life:

May the God before whom my fathers Abraham and Isaac walked, the God who has been my shepherd all my life to this day, the Angel who has delivered me from all harm....

Beautiful, isn't it? At the time of our death, as our days come to a close, we too need to take Jacob's lead and use that moment to build the last of our altars here on earth: altars of worship, praise and adoration. We will never walk this way again—what a great incentive, then, while we pass this way, to build an 'altar' of worship to God.

I have not quite decided on my own yet. Probably, when the time comes, it will be the song most relevant to me then. If it had been at the period during which my dad died, it would have been *You are my hiding place.* If it were to happen now, it would be *Faithful One.* Perhaps, when it is my turn to die, it will be *Great is the Lord.*

Even as death approached, Jacob took the opportunity to praise God. May we do likewise.

WITH A HEART FOR OTHERS [Genesis 49:29–33]
When my dad died, I asked a very good friend of mine to conduct the funeral. My one request to him was that he preach the gospel. I told him that if he did not, then *I* would get up there and do it! Of course, we cannot ever say with certainty that anyone has not, at the last, met Jesus Christ, repented, and turned to him, but to the best of my knowledge, my father was not a believer. I knew that many of his friends, relatives, and past workmates were also unbelievers. In all probability, they would never hear the gospel preached other than at that moment. It was too late for my dad, but it was not too late for the others. Yes, the officiant could give a consoling word to the family, but that could come later, back at the house. At the crematorium it was time to preach the gospel.

The last days of Jacob on earth, and the events that surrounded his death, were marked by ministry to others. Jacob ministered God's word and promises. How? By giving his blessing to his own family and by attempting to influence spiritually the growing Hebrew community which, for the last seventeen years, had been resident in Egypt—a period, Jacob thought, which could have caused them to forget where it was that they had come from.

Jacob did not know how long remained for the Hebrews to live in Egypt. What he did know was that the occasion of his death gave him the opportunity to remind them all, powerfully, that they were not of Egypt but rather of Canaan, the Promised Land. Jacob had Joseph swear that he would be buried in the same place as Abraham and Isaac. All of them, every Israelite, would leave Egypt and see the homeland. They would all go to bury Jacob, the patriarchal father. They would walk the Promised Land, see its sites and breathe its air.

I read recently about a retired college professor who arranged with one of his former students, whom he was now mentoring, how his funeral should be conducted—particularly what should be said and done. One of the requests was that, at the end of the talk, as the eternal resting place that was his and ours was spoken about, the former student was to take the professor's walking cane, by which everyone knew him, and break it in two—an act which was intended to dramatically symbolise the great hope that is ours. As he had in life, so in his death, that professor wanted to minister to those who were left behind.

To minister to others in his time of dying—that was Jacob's desire. It should be our desire, too. It often marks the deaths of those who *die well*. We do not need to be concerned about great eulogies; nor should we worry about making sure that people get a good feed! What matters is that people will walk out differently after having come to pay their last respects.

WITH A HOUSE IN ORDER

Recently, I received a letter from a friend. In the midst of telling me all that he was up to at the moment, he commented that one of his friends, with whom he has a weekly Bible study, had just been diagnosed with a terminal illness. Consequently, his friend was active at the moment, putting his house in order. In the midst of all the planning that needed to go on; in the midst of living his final few days, saying his goodbyes, the dying man was active in contacting people, sorting out everything that he felt was undone in his life.

Jacob did this, too. From the account of his final days, we can see that he set about putting his house in order, in both the physical and the spiritual senses. This meant wrapping up any outstanding things from the past, and ensuring that everything was in place for the future. Perhaps the latter is an area that we are often blind to.

We see Jacob setting about this task in three ways. Firstly, he incorporates Joseph's boys into his family. [See 48:17–20.] As Joseph's sons, they would share in the family inheritance back in the Promised Land, but as Jacob's grandsons, they would only inherit a portion. Jacob, believing that Joseph was key to the purposes of God, took it upon himself to legally upgrade their relationship with himself to the status of adoptive sons. They would then be treated as if they were his. What is interesting about this incorporation is that it was done in a way which initially offended Joseph. The younger one was blessed first by Jacob, and thereby given the more prominent role in the future. Despite Joseph's protests, it seems that Jacob had received a divine command that it should be so. Jacob's faithfulness to God's word was such that he would not be swayed or influenced: he knew precisely what God had told him to do, concerning the way he was to administer the blessing. Even now, at the last, he was determined to do things God's way, even if the family found this hard to take.

Secondly, Jacob gave Joseph and his boys a piece of land in Canaan. [See 48:22.] When Jacob got this land we are not told. At all events, this represented an act of faith that one day they would be in Canaan again; Jacob was keen that Joseph should have this gift.

Thirdly, when he has gathered all his boys together, Jacob gives them the special family blessing. It is an interesting mix of judgement, prayerful prophecies, reward for good sonship, and supernatural revelations. There is the declaration of judgement on Simeon for sleeping with his father's concubine, and for the two lads who ransacked the village of Dinah's rapist. There is reward: one of Joseph's boys would become the major clan. There was supernatural revelation: out of Judah would come the Messiah.

113

HERE LIES GOD'S MAN

What is the application of all this for us? As it had been with
Abraham, so it was with Isaac; as it was now with Jacob, so it
would be one day, very soon, with his offspring. Jacob's house is
put in order in a way that accords with what God has said He is
doing and going to do in the future. Those who are dying are
often encouraged to sort things out. They frequently do make
plans and decisions according to their own views and their wishes
for others. A Christian should be looking, above all, at God's
purposes, and His commands.

The greatest command of love means that in all we do to 'set
our house in order' we will both express the love, and reflect the
wisdom of our heavenly Father.

We can pray to Him to give us that wisdom, so that we have
gospel priorities at the heart of this final decision making process.

Perhaps we can leave instructions which will help the funeral
itself to be a moment when the gospel is shared, and joy in the
resurrection expressed.

We may have the means to provide for some Christian work to
be supported from our estate, as well as making proper provision
for the family.

But, most importantly, we can ask for forgiveness where
appropriate; making sure we have given forgiveness wherever that
is needed; ensuring that we are right with God.

In the whole process, the God whose love for you is
demonstrated by the passion of the Cross will be with you, as He
has been all along the way.   He will still be *for* you; He will be
leading you; His promises are for you, personally—and that
amazing personal relationship you have with Him will never cease.
Your awareness of it will grow until you come into His presence,
finally, to enjoy Him for ever.

When I was brought up in the Brethren, there was a song around
that expressed the great work that God had done and was doing in
our lives. It went something like this:

> *What a wonderful change in my life has been wrought,*
> *since Jesus came into my heart,*
> *since Jesus came into my heart,*
> *since Jesus came into my heart,*
> *floods of joy, O my soul, like the sea billows roll,*
> *since Jesus came into my heart.*

All those centuries before the incarnation of Jesus, the Son of God, the same truth was nonetheless at work. This is a great mystery, but we know that God is faithful and His nature is unchanging. The great saints of the Old Testament knew God's personal reality, even though the full and final revelation in Jesus Christ had not yet been explicitly given. So it is entirely appropriate to say that the life-changing work of God in a human being which is expressed in that song was accomplished in Jacob. There is one Holy Spirit, whose work in creation is proclaimed from the opening of Genesis to the end of Revelation. There is a unity and continuity about the witness of the Bible, on this as on every matter. The faithfulness of Jacob, in a very different age from ours, set in the Old Testament period, whereas we live under the new covenant, is nonetheless powerfully relevant for us—because, at the last, he displayed that gift of faith which is the sure sign of the Spirit of God at work.

We see redemption: for Jacob had at one time been the deceiver, known as such throughout the family. But now, at a ripe old age, he was going to meet his maker as *Israel*, one who wrestles with God and has overcome. The tests and trials were over now—as, one day, they shall be for us. He had lived a life that had seen him changed into a completely new person, with new hopes, new priorities, new faith and a new love. That can be our testimony, too. Our God is the same today—He is the life-changing God, and He is the God who communicates His purposes, not like dumb idols, false deities and new age myths.

What a wonderful thing has been wrought in my life, since Jesus came into my heart. May God, through the work of the Holy Spirit, change, and go on changing your life, today and every day, so that when the moment comes to go and be with our Lord in heaven, a song of praise may be on our lips, and on the lips of all those who will gather to mark our passing.

PRAYER

Heavenly Father, in preparation for my last
days on this earth, cause me to be one who is
continually building altars of worship.
When the hour of my death draws near,
help me to be ready to leave this world
with faith in you for the future;
thankfulness for your involvement in my life;
with a heart for others, and with my house in order.

Grant me the blessing of a good death,
marked by faith, not fear;
and, until that time comes,
help me to walk your way in obedience,
with confidence in your promises.

AFTERWORD

AFTERWORD

The matter of death may seem remote. It has become almost an unmentionable, or impolite, subject. Our society fosters an illusion that this life just goes on and on.... But I urge you that if you know, deep down, there is unfinished business you still have to complete with Jesus Christ, do it today! He said, *I am the way and the truth and the life. No one comes to the Father except through me* [John 14:6]. Will you take him at his word and follow him as your Lord and Saviour? He awaits your decision. It is a decision for now.

It is an alarming and maybe a horrifying truth, but it might be the one thing you really need to know: that tomorrow could be too late. Do not put off, even for a moment longer, the most vital transaction of life. It is a simple one: He offers you everything— forgiveness of all sin, assurance of salvation to eternal life, a peace that passes all understanding. What he asks from you is everything. You must personally accept Jesus Christ, the Son of God, who died on the Cross of Calvary to pay the penalty of your sin. From the moment you do receive him, you will *remain in him* and he will *remain in you*, according to his promise. [See John 15:4.] Do not believe those who say this is unnecessary, for *no one can see the kingdom of God unless he is born again* [John 3:3]. *And if anyone does not have the Spirit of Christ, he does not belong to Christ* [Romans 8:9b].

God is not cruel. His nature is love. He does not will that anyone should spend eternity apart from Him. He desires that you will respond in repentance to His loving offer in Jesus. But He will never force you to accept. The option is open to reject the divine offer. Judgement is real. Hell is real, too; and it awaits those who are relying upon their own merits, for all have sinned and gone astray from the perfect law of love.

So ensure, above all, that you have received Christ as your personal Saviour and Lord. Then you will not only have the one essential for a 'good death', whatever its time or place may be; you will be acquitted on the great Day of Judgement, for you will have been washed perfectly clean by the blood of Jesus. You will enjoy an eternity of loving fellowship with Jesus, in company with all the saints, because his merit is then yours as his free gift; and his victory over evil is yours, too, as his gift to you. What could be better than that?

Paul Griffiths Ministries

bringing God to people

Paul Griffiths Ministries is a charity that exists to bring God to people. Started in 1997, it has begun to fulfil its purpose in the following ways:

☐   Sponsoring a daily evangelistic broadcast across the Caribbean and Europe with TransWorld Radio, entitled *God on Life*.

☐   Promoting and running a faith-sharing training course called *Telling our Story*.

☐   Co-ordinating a Bible School for Christians in the Forest of Dean and South Wales areas.

☐   Releasing evangelistic and Bible teaching material. The first of these was an evangelistic booklet called *The God of Hope*.

☐   The itinerant Bible teaching and evangelistic ministry of Paul Griffiths.

With regard to the future, the charity would like to establish a Hospitality House, providing a holiday ministry for people in full-time work, and run evangelistic missions and evangelism training courses for those in church leadership.

Further information about the activities of Paul Griffiths Ministries can be obtained from visiting our website:

http://www.PaulGriffithsMinistries.org.uk

or write to Paul Griffiths at:

Paul Griffiths Ministries
PO Box 31, Lydney, Glos. GL15 6YP UK

Charity Number 1067753